FOOTBALL'S GREATEST INSULTS

Compiled and Written by

Kevin Nelson

A Perigee Book

To Scott Thomason, a truly great sports fan.

Perigee Books
are published by
The Putnam Publishing Group
200 Madison Avenue
New York, NY 10016

Library of Congress Cataloging-in-Publication Data

Football's greatest insults / compiled and written by Kevin Nelson.
p. cm.
ISBN 0-399-51688-3 (trade pbk.)
1. Football—United States—Quotations, maxims, etc.   I. Nelson, Kevin,
date.
GV959.F58   1991   91–12577 CIP
796.332'0973—dc20

Cover design by Bob Silverman

Printed in the United States of America
1 2 3 4 5 6 7 8 9 10

This book is printed on acid-free paper.
∞

Contents

Foreword

No B.S.

That's the best thing about football.

That's not to say there isn't plenty of B.S. in the game. Just listen to the NFL propaganda machine any Sunday or the television hypemasters and you'll get lots and lots of it.

But the game in its best and purest form has nothing to do with what they're trying to sell you on TV.

Basically, it's this: Strap on the pads, and bang heads. The team that blocks and tackles and bangs heads with fierce, nut-cracking abandon is going to be the team that wins the game. Everything else is bunk.

This book, *Football's Greatest Insults,* is dedicated to puncturing some of the pomposities that have grown up around the game. This is not the picture presented to you on those Sunday afternoon highlights shows where, as someone has pointed out, the deep-throated announcer sounds like he's doing play-by-play for the Allied invasion of Normandy.

This is not the techno-militaristic, pseudo-scientific, super-complicated, jargon-heavy, expertly analyzed sport that so many people try to make it.

This is guys screaming at each other. This is players insulting their coaches and teammates squabbling with one another. This is owners hissing at each other like alley cats. This is the fans dumping on the dumb coach and the dumber owner. This is players and coaches hacked off at the lousy, fair-weather fans. This is players talking trash at the media, and the media talking trash back at them.

This is what you don't get when the TV cameras are rolling. The three f's: fussin', feudin' and fightin'. And you can put cursing and bitching and moaning and back-stabbing in there, too.

There will be no advertisements for the United Way in this

book. No sincere-looking nose tackles with 19-inch necks who can't read themselves talking about literacy programs in their areas. No players who spit blood on Sundays talking about how much they love little children and dogs.

No B.S.

That's the goal of this book. Have some laughs, kick dirt on as many overblown reputations as we can find, and keep the B.S. quotient as low as possible.

A few housekeeping matters: As much as I believe the author should get as much credit as possible for putting this book together, lots of other people have contributed, whether they know it or not. Among them are: Scott Ostler, Mike Lupica, Tony Kornheiser, Lowell Cohn, Mike Littwin, Tom Fitzgerald, Ira Kamin, Frank Blackman, Frank Cooney, Norman Chad, Rick Reilly, David Harris. These guys (except for Harris) are sportswriters. As such, they are among the finest human beings on this planet. Their work has helped make this book the glorious thing it is, and if I don't mention their names up front one of them might seek me out and stab me with a pencil.

Another point. Obviously, things change, even in football. Players change teams, retire, die. But when a player or coach is quoted here, he is usually identified according to the team he was with at the time of the remark. And that may not be the team he happens to be with now.

Who cares, right? Agreed. One of the biggest problems with pro football is that we load it up with so much garbage the week before that the game itself can't help but be a letdown. We'll not make that mistake here.

Enough with the prefatory material! Let the head-banging begin!

—Kevin Nelson

1

Glamour Boys: All About the Guys Who Throw the Ball, Get the Chicks and Have Great Hair

Let's talk quarterbacks. The guys who handle the ball. Who get the chicks and the big-bucks contracts. The guys who get to sell Isotoner gloves and Diet Pepsi on TV. They're the glamour pusses of the game, and Art Donovan, an NFL tackle from long ago, has got them pegged right. Tell us about it, Fatso:

"Show me a quarterback today, and I'll show you a surfer. They got a bunch of beauties now. This guy Troy Aikman—they gave him $11.2 million before the guy ever threw a pass in the NFL. But he's like the rest of them. He and Elway and Montana—they all look like they should be out on the Pacific Ocean, hanging ten."

It's like it isn't good enough if you can throw a pass a mile and run like a deer. You've got to be blond and blue-eyed too, or you just aren't going to make it in the pros. Look at Aikman, for instance. Couldn't cut it at Oklahoma so he transferred to UCLA. Of course they let him in. He had blond hair. It's mandatory for all UCLA students.

Now he's with the Cowboys after Dallas decided to stick with him and ship his young, high-priced backup, Steve Walsh, over to the Saints. The Saints were in desperate need—it's a permanent condition with them—because they had John Fourcade taking the snaps.

"To call John Fourcade an average quarterback would be giving him all the best of it. Any time he threw further than 10 yards last night, he was throwing it up for grabs."
—Lowell Cohn, sports columnist

The protypical blond surfer quarterback, John Elway.

Maybe Fourcade's problem was that he doesn't have blond hair. The NFL's PR police wouldn't allow it. Sorry, buddy. Either stand a little closer to the peroxide or you're outta here. League rules.

Actually, no. Fourcade's problem wasn't his hair (not having any never hurt Terry Bradshaw, right?)—it was the fact that, as a quarterback, he stunk. But you gotta like the guy anyway because when Walsh came over in that big deal in '90, John didn't lie down and play dead.

Said John: "Basically Steve Walsh is coming in here with just his college statistics. Sure he won a national championship, but this isn't college and these aren't the Miami Hurricanes."

That's right, John. We've seen the Miami Hurricanes, and most years they could whip the pants off the Saints. But that's another story. Right now we're exploring why so many blond airhead surfer types are now collecting paychecks as quarterbacks of the NFL. Here's another: John Elway.

Okay, okay. So maybe Elway's not an airhead. He graduated from Stanford which, after all, still ranks higher than Walsh's alma mater academically, although not in the production of national football championships in the 1980s. Stanford is known, however, for producing fine quarterbacks, and Elway is in a long line that includes Sid Luckman, John Brodie and Jim Plunkett.

The rap against Elway is that he's never won a Super Bowl—or even come close—but that wasn't why the Broncos QB got into such hot water a couple of years ago. Elway, who's bigger in Denver than Madonna, got ticked off because reporters were prying into what candy he gave out for Halloween, and he spilled his guts to a *Sports Illustrated* reporter:

"The bottom line is, I want to be able to go out and have a drink somewhere, whether it's a Coca-Cola or a Coors Light. I'd like for my daughters to be able to give out candy without Denver knowing what we're giving out. That's something I'm getting fed up with."

Pretty mild stuff really, but from the reaction in Denver you'd have thought that the Elways were spiking that candy with LSD. From Jay Mariotti, a local columnist:

"This person [Elway] isn't Denver's finest resource. He's a greedy and scared punk who has been pampered so long his senses are askew. He is a hypocrite in the worst way, a public figure who makes all the money he can from his celebrity and screams the spotlight is too hot."

After it was suggested that Elway might be so burned out on Denver that he'd ask for a trade, Mariotti added:

"Go ahead, John. Leave. Get out of Denver, baby, go. You'll be crawling back here after a week."

At that year's Super Bowl—the Broncs got creamed, natch—the issue of Elway's maturity came up again, and this time Terry Bradshaw, the shiny-headed former quarterback, got into the act, blowing a big raspberry at Elway:

"John's been babied, babied by the city, until this year when they jumped his ass. And he's been babied by the coaching staff. He's had it too easy. . . . He's too, too inconsistent. Things bother John more than they bother Joe [Montana]. He's worried about his Mercedes-Benz, about candy bars. And John's got to get more tough emotionally, mentally. He's making $2 million a year. Things like that shouldn't bother you if you're making $2 million a year."

After Bradshaw's remarks were circulated around Bourbon Street, Broncos receiver Vance Johnson rose to his teammate's defense:

"It sounds to me like a jealous man. Why would Bradshaw say something like that? John must have beat him at golf."

And Elway himself responded to the challenge:

"Terry's been saying that all through my career. He's jealous of my money. He's jealous of my hair."

See? What were we saying? It all comes back to hair. Joe Montana has pretty good hair, although it's thinning a little in front. (It's true, Joe. You can't hide it.) And he's shown what's left of it in so many commercials he's almost putting Arnold Palmer to shame. It's amazing, about these big-time jocks. They're supposed to be role models for America, people whom our children can admire and emulate. But they'll sell anything. Wave enough dough in front of a superstar's face, and he'll pitch your product with the ham-handed glee of a used-car salesman.

Along with all the money he makes, Montana has practically been raised to sainthood—Saint Joseph, patron saint of Super Bowl titles—by his legions of abject admirers.

"Few Americans are revered in quite the way that sports stars are. After reading *Sports Illustrated*'s latest paean to Joe Montana, the quarterback of the San Francisco 49ers ("An 11½-year-old named Matthew Hart had a brain tumor. . . . The meeting lasted 45 minutes . . . Joe left. Matt's crisis passed."), all that is left to hear about the great man are the details of the virgin birth."

—The Economist

Defensive tackles are not quite as worshipful, however. Another more serious problem for the aging Montana has been his rapidly decreasing mobility which, despite his four Super Bowl rings, is increasingly being commented upon by the large, beefy men trying to run him down:

"Randall Cunningham is the best athlete in NFL history to play that position. I'd much rather play against an old guy like Joe Montana. He goes down when you breathe on him."

—Steve McMichael, Bears defensive tackle

"If you get close to Montana, he will go down. He doesn't like to take a vicious hit. You try to take the quick route to him. You're not looking to sack him. You're just looking to rush him."

—Lawrence Taylor, Giants linebacker

"It's his receivers. I'd say they're the best we've ever played against. Definitely. When you throw a three-yard pass the way Montana does and then the receiver runs 12 yards, I could do that."

—Henry Thomas, defensive tackle

It's worth noting that Henry Thomas made his comment after his Vikings had just been shellacked by the 49ers in a playoff game, something which has frequently happened to opponents of Montana, dink passes or no. But that's life for a pro quarterback. For Montana and for all the rest of them. Even when you win, some folks are going to put the knock on you.

After Jim Everett engineered a masterful down-the-field drive in the final quarter to set up a field goal that beat the 49ers, a reporter asked cornerback Eric Wright what he thought of the Rams' signal-caller:

"He had a good game. So what? He didn't do anything to catch my eye."

Okay, Eric. So you're not easily impressed. Which figures. You were a defensive guy, and the people who are least impressed by quarterbacks are defensive guys, especially defensive-line guys. Linemen just hate quarterbacks. They hate the fact that the girls in the stands all know the quarterback's name but that nobody but their mothers and grandmothers know who they are, or care. They hate how they can be playing a game and while they're bleeding and filthy dirty and one finger is hanging disconnected from when that Bozo in the pile bit it, the quarterback's jersey looks like it was handwashed in a mountain stream by virgins. They hate everything about those effete, sweet-smelling, headline-hogging quarterbacks. They hate, yes, even their hair.

Listen to one lineman (Fred Smerlas) talk about a pair of quarterbacks he faced when he was with the Bills. First, Tony Eason:

"The consummate crumble guy. When I think of him, the first image that comes to mind is that chickenshit look he always has on his face. It's as if he knows he's going to get mauled. And he wants no part of it. He's the kind of quarterback a defensive lineman hopes won't ever get yanked or carried off the field. You almost feel like giving him part of your salary for making you look so good."

And next, Ken O'Brien:

"Another Jet I wouldn't mind facing on a weekly basis. Instead of doing the I'm-too-young-to-die two-step, he does something equally beneficial to defenders by sitting in the pocket and taking sacks. . . . From what I could see, his protection wasn't nearly as bad as he made it look by holding the ball too long."

And O'Brien probably wasn't nearly as bad as his old nemesis made him out to be. But that's the way it is with linemen. Any chance they get to goof on a QB, they'll take it. Like when lineman-turned-labor boss Gene Upshaw was in Miami for a TV interview. He thought he was off the air when he started joking about Vinny Testaverde, one of Florida's finest scholar-athletes since graduated to the pros:

"I'm better than Testaverde. . . . Testaverde is so dumb he would drag the electric cord through his swimming pool while clipping the hedges."

Appalled by this remark, Bucs coach Ray Perkins questioned Upshaw's own brain capacity:

"Anyone who would say things like that is a person in need of an IQ transplant."

Quarterbacks are supposed to have it all: good looks, brains, money, a beautiful wife and kids, and the God-given talent to throw a queer-shaped leather object through a tire 75 yards away. It's understandable that many of our contemporary standard-bearers do not quite live up to this lofty ideal. Like Vinny Testaverde, Bubby Brister is attacked for his intelligence, or lack of same:

"They've got to be awfully hard-pressed for good candy bars in Pittsburgh to name one after an idiot like Bubby Brister. Bubby's IQ has never hit room temperature."
—Ralph Barbieri, radio host

But truth be told, when things were going bad for Bubby in Pittsburgh, they dumped on him for just about everything. Defensive end Ray Childress called him "an arrogant little punk," and a Pittsburgh radio station got a lot of play out of a song entitled, "Mamas Don't Let Your Bubbys Grow Up To Be QBs." And when things really went to hell for Bubby they started telling a joke around town about how he had taken to sleeping at Three Rivers Stadium. Yessiree. It seems Bubby painted the door of his apartment to look like an end zone, and after that he couldn't find it.

They put the squeeze on Randall Cunningham for being, get this, an *athlete.* Somebody who can do something besides drop back five yards and fling it.

"He's an athlete, not a quarterback."
—Terry Bradshaw

Read between the lines and what Terry is really saying is that Randall isn't smart, can't read defenses, and doesn't have a clue about leading the team—in other words, all the things they used to say about Bradshaw when he was young.

. Then there's Mike Tomczak. A tough, hard-nosed player, by most standards. But unfortunately for Mike, quarterbacks don't lead with their noses.

"I'm not a big fan of Mike Tomczak. He sometimes shows the field generalship of Pee-Wee Herman."
—Randy Cross, ex-49er center

"Tomczak looks like the Karate Kid. When he comes off the field after a bad pass, I keep expecting Mr. Miyagi to be on the sidelines."
—Fred Smerlas

Bubby Brister, said one defensive end, is "an arrogant little punk,"

Jay Schroeder started his career with the Redskins, but it's probably inevitable that he would wind up in California playing for the Raiders. He's another one of Fatso Donovan's blond, "Surf's Up!" quarterback clones, and when he came to the 'Skins Joe Theismann, his predecessor at quarterback, wasn't too impressed. Said Joe:

"What you're seeing is what you got. He's not any better or worse than what you see. He's a sub-50 percent passer, and he'll probably throw six interceptions for every four touchdown passes."

As a member of the Silver and Black, Jay seems to have matured as a flinger of footballs, but some still aren't convinced:

"Schroeder may be improved, but he's still as dynamic as a parked car. He looks good on a play-action pass after one of Bo Jackson's 88-yard runs. But if the Raiders fall behind . . . you may want to send the children from the room. Schroeder could go hours without hitting a human being with a pass."
—Gary Peterson, sports columnist

Then there's that new game based on Schroeder's passing skills, as explained by C. W. Nevius: "The name-the-receiver-Jay Schroeder-was-actually-throwing-to game. For experts only."

Still, almost everybody, including his Raider teammates, would agree that Schroeder is a step up from the spindly legged weenie he replaced as quarterback, Marc Wilson:

"You know the difference between those two guys? My personal gut feeling? I knew Jay was trying to do better. Wilson, I didn't think he was trying to improve his game. He had a ticket to ride and he rode it out. . . . Wilson, we saw the same mistakes time after time after time, year after year after year."
—Greg Townsend, Raiders lineman

In fairness to Wilson, though, quarterbacks are like presidents. They get too much credit when things are going good, and too much blame when they turn sour. Lefty quarterback Boomer Esiason—another friggin' blond!—took his Bengals to the Super Bowl in 1989, but when he hit a bad patch a couple of seasons later the vultures came out to roost:

"I think he's a loser."
—Andy Furman, Cincinnati talk show host

"I think what you're seeing is the real Boomer. I think before, he may have been playing over his head."
—Former NFL player,
as quoted in *The Sporting News*

Fact is, the role of quarterback is overblown. If the Bengals turned into cream cheese, it wasn't just Boomer's fault. Everybody on the team had a hand in it. But quarterbacks are the center of attention, and so this big mystique has gathered around the position and the men who play it.

"Quarterbacks aren't gods, not even with a small g. They aren't as important now as they were a decade or two ago, and in the future they'll probably be even less important."

—Fran Tarkenton, former quarterback

And take it from Terry Bradshaw, who should know. It isn't even that difficult to do.

"Heck, what is there to quarterbacking? If a receiver's open, throw it to him. If he's not open, throw it to him anyway. Let the guy show his athletic ability."

2

Genius This Year, Bum the Next: The Ups and Downs of Being a Football Coach

"There are only two things in coaching," said Chuck Knox. "One is winning, the other is misery." Ain't that the truth. A football coach leads the life of a manic-depressive: One Sunday he's flying high as the clouds; the next Sunday he's in the gutter waving a bottle of Thunderbird around and singing, "Nobody loves me but my mama, and she could be jivin' me, too."

Up and down, down and up, and you're only as good as your last game, as the old saw goes.

Jimmy Johnson of the Cowboys will vouch for this. When he first came into the league, replacing the immortal stone-face, Tom Landry, you'd have thought he wanted to redecorate the Alamo in salmon pink and sea-foam gray judging from the reactions of Texans.

"Buying the Cowboys and replacing Tom Landry is like buying a dream house and filling in the swimming pool to plant radishes."
—Kevin Lamb, sportswriter

The big gripe against Johnson was that he came from a college program. Many dyed-in-the-wool NFL types think that the rah-rah, sis-boom-bah techniques that may have worked on campus just won't cut in in the pros.

"How many college guys have ever made it? Not one. I mean, really made it. Look at the record. Bud Wilkinson couldn't do it and John McKay couldn't do it. You want to win in this man's league, you find yourself a good NFL assistant."
—Buddy Ryan

"This league eats up legends and myths. It just chews them up. This league eats up phonies. I've seen some college football people

who have never made it through a year here; this league will come after you. How many have come and gone as quick as an eyelash?"
—Jerry Glanville

Both Glanville and Ryan slogged away for a long time in the NFL assistant ranks before getting a shot at the top job, so that may explain their bias. Johnson was coach at the University of Miami, although it may be stretching things a little to call that "a college program." In fact Johnson's college opponents used to gripe, as Randy Galloway has pointed out, that his Miami teams were "paid better than some NFL clubs." Besides coming from the colleges, which was bad enough, Johnson compounded his early problems by having bad hair.

"I would like to lay to rest forever the silly notion that Dallas Cowboy coach Jimmy Johnson's hair doesn't move. While watching the Cowboys-Eagles game on December 10, I distinctly saw one of Johnson's hairs move while he was animatedly complaining to one of the officials. I think it was the hair growing out of follicle number 4317 in the front left quadrant."
—Letter-writer to the Sporting Green of the
San Francisco Chronicle

A newspaper reported that Johnson worked 18 hours a day as coach. "That's impossible," said Glanville. "It takes him 12 hours to comb his hair." In order to taunt the Cowboys during a game against them, Glanville's Falcons broke their huddles by saying, in unison, "Hairspray!" It must have worked because the Falcons won the game.

Even members of the Cowboys spoke up on the hair issue:

"If he [Johnson] wanted me to run 26 miles through hills, I would. If he wanted me to carry water bottles, I would. If he wanted me to go to the barber and get my hair cut like his, well, you have to draw the line somewhere."
—Babe Laufenberg, backup quarterback

The anti-Johnson faction in the NFL (which is sizable) was confirmed in their suspicions after his rookie year in Dallas, which was as ghastly as his haircut.

"I was shocked. But that's how it was in Dallas. One week Joe Blockhead would come in and play. The next week it would be Willie Whoever. It was fantasy football, picking names for the week and letting the chips fall. More often than not, the chips fell on top of us."

—Paul Palmer, running back for the Cowboys
during Johnson's first year

The Cowboys stunk up the joint in 1989 and got buried most every week. After losing their first three games, a Dallas TV reporter joked: "Sunday Silence is the horse named after the Cowboys' offense." Texans—who never much liked the idea of a guy from Florida coming in to tell *them* about football anyway—called Johnson's hiring "The Dawn of a New Error." The joke around Dallas was that the Cowboys were like maxi-pads—good for one period. At an NFL meeting Johnson tried to avoid reporters by climbing down the fire escape from the 11th floor of his hotel. One observer noted that it was the fastest the Cowboys had moved all season.

There were reports of dissension among Cowboy players, who mocked Johnson's coaching style as being too much in the schoolboy college vein. After a tough loss to the Cardinals, Johnson erupted at Everson Walls for talking to St. Louis receiver Roy Green as they left the field, and Walls and his coach ended up in a yelling match. Said a disgusted Walls:

"I was only doing what about 20 other players were doing. That was embarrassing. That only happens with college coaches and Mike Ditka."

Before that Cardinals game, Dallas linebacker Eugene Lockhart said he wouldn't have sex until the winless Cowboys got a victory. After the game a Phoenix player said, "The way they're going, he could be celibate a long time." And so it went for Dallas the entire sex-starved '89 season.

Then what happened? It turned around the next year. The Cowboys almost get into the playoffs, Herschel Walker goes to the Vikings for a knapsack full of draft choices, Troy Aikman looks like the real thing at quarterback, they win some tough games against good opponents, and suddenly Jimmy Johnson is a lacquer-haired genius. Who needs Tom Landry anyway? But you can count on one thing: As soon as the Cowboys go bad, Johnson will become a bum again.

Another guy who's been tagged with the "genius" label is Sam Wyche who, despite coaching two Super Bowl teams, was called "a social leper" by one Cincinnati paper. Some have derided his innovative offensive schemes as "popcorn football" and implied they were too complicated for simple-minded football players:

"Do the benefits of the no-huddle offense outweigh the busted assignments it causes? You can give a football player too much to think about."

—Mike Dodd, *Cincinnati Enquirer*

Nowadays, of course, the no-huddle offense is widely employed around the NFL, a tribute to Wyche's "genius." And so it goes—a coach's reputation roller coasting up and down depending on what the win-loss column says. John Robinson of the Rams is praised for his conservative, ball control approach when he's winning; a few losses in a row and he has, in the words of one writer, "all the imagination of an avocado." The same holds doubly true for Bill Parcells. Do the Giants play boring football, or what? But as long as you win a Super Bowl every four or five years, who's gonna complain?

Mike Ditka has had his fling with the genius thing, too. After his Bears won everything in sight in 1986, he was a man's man, a coach's coach, the quintessential football personality. Then came the heart attack, more disputes with Jim McMahon and other stars from '86, tough losses to the 49ers and Giants, injuries to key players until, finally, the utter collapse of the team three years later. "At the end of last season [1989] a lot of our guys probably would have rather voted for Saddam Hussein as Man of the Year rather than Coach," said Dan Hampton.

That 1989 season probably marked the nadir of Ditka's career as a coach. One of Big Mike's charms is that he has always been willing to call a spade a spade. His assessments of his 1987 Bears in mid-season—"We stink"—and of his 1988 squad are prime examples:

"We don't have any good players here. We have a lot of old guys who limp out and try to play and a lot of young guys who help carry them out."

But 1989 provided a much richer landscape for Ditka's talent for invective. After the Redskins clobbered the Bears, handing the proud franchise of Halas, Butkus and Sayers one of the most embarrassing losses in its history, Ditka erupted,

"This is absolutely the worst exhibition of football I've ever seen. We stink. We are an absolutely atrocious football team at

Mike Ditka, says one former NFL great, "reminds me of many of the coaches back in the NFL in the 1950s: fascist, loud . . . but not exactly Phi Beta Kappa."

this point. We have to play the rest of our games, but there's no question in my mind that we will be fortunate to win one game."

Asked by a reporter if maybe Washington didn't deserve some credit for beating the Bears, Ditka pounded it in some more: "I absolutely refuse to give credit to the other team because we stink. We're an atrocious football team." He added that rookie cornerback Donnell Woolford "evidently can't cover anybody" and went on to say,

"We had no pressure. We can't play man-to-man. Our pass coverage was terrible. We just can't play. There's nothing we can do this year about it. I think it's over."

Well, he was right. The Bears lost the four games they played after that and ten of their last 12. But many observers wondered if Ditka himself hadn't brought his team down with his incessant ranting and raving.

"He has shown himself to be a front-running coach. He's relatively normal when things are going well, but he disintegrates in the face of adversity. For all his Bear-like growling, Ditka does not seem to have the inner grace to handle a failing situation. He makes it worse."

—Lowell Cohn, columnist

"[Ditka] reminds me of many of the coaches back in the NFL of the 1950s: fascist, loud . . . but not exactly Phi Beta Kappa."
—Jim Brown, former star running back

Wondering who might replace Ditka as coach, Chicago columnist Terry Boers suggested convicted hotel princess Leona Helmsley: "Coach Leona Helmsley—mean, spiteful and loves to treat people like dirt, so she'd fit right in."

One of the uglier episodes in Ditka's coaching career occurred at Candlestick Park in San Francisco after a humiliating Monday night whipping at the hands of the 49ers. Irked not only by the loss but also by the taunts he was receiving from fans, he hurled his chewing gum into the stands and hit a woman spectator. The San Francisco papers wanted to see Ditka lashed to the stake, but his fellow Chicagoans were more supportive, attacking the woman for being a rowdy:

"Most likely, she was among the fans who were braying at Ditka. . . . They weren't satisfied with merely winning. They had to rub it in by squealing 'Nya, nya' or 'Poo to you' or 'Tee hee.' Those are the sort of things Frisco fans say, you know. I don't mean to offend that city's football enthusiasts, but the fact is, they're sissies. They are the only fans in the nation who blow kisses at players."

—Mike Royko, columnist

Royko attacked San Francisco fans for being pansies. But a Los Angeles columnist who knows Candlestick better attacked San Francisco fans (more properly) for acting like thugs:

"The question for San Francisco now is this: Isn't it time for your sports fans to take that one big step up the ladder of evolution? Leave the cave? For years the Candlestick Park crowds, baseball and football, have been among the nastiest, sloppiest, most inane and confrontational. . . . The lady who allegedly was struck on the head with the flying gum is considering legal action. Good luck. With a Candlestick Park fan, it might be very difficult to assess the exact cause of brain damage."

—Scott Ostler

Ditka himself (probably on the advice of lawyers) had nothing much to say about this incident, but on most other matters he is hardly the shy and retiring type. He once criticized Bengals running back James Brooks as a has-been, and in their game against the Bears, Brooks made a 28-yard run in which he was shoved out of bounds into the coach. There was quite an impact, and it knocked Ditka's sunglasses into the air. Asked if the collision was accidental, Brooks said,

"What we saw was a guy who runs his mouth and deserved to get it smacked. Mike Ditka is a fat-headed redneck."

Brooks is right, of course. Ditka *is* a fat-headed redneck, but coaching football is one of the few professions—Marine drill sergeant is another—where you can be a fat-headed redneck and get away with it. It's very nearly part of the job description, in fact. But if you're gonna be a fat-headed redneck you might as well be a good one, and Ditka certainly is that. When he is P.O.'d is when he produces some of his best stuff.

Such as when Otis Wilson, a member of that great '86 Bear team who had since moved on to the Raiders, commented that Chicago wasn't as intimidating as it used to be. Ditka didn't much appreciate this and launched into a long tirade insulting Wilson's intelligence:

"Well, nobody ever gave him a Phi Beta Kappa award, did they? I wouldn't worry too much about what Otis observed. He better observe trying to make the football team. If they want to sling shots, we'll sling shots. I'll put my record up against anybody's, including his. When you have people who become disgruntled and take cheap shots after the fact, it's kind of interesting. But consider the source. In everything in life, if you consider the source, you should have no problems. And that's why I have no problems with it, because the source is absolutely nothing."

Following his heart attack in 1988, Ditka has tried, with limited success, to remain calm and avoid these sorts of outbursts, for he knows that in order to survive as a coach in the NFL, you must, of course, remain alive. Or do you? There is the curious case of Joe Walton. Alive . . . or dead? Although he served as head coach of their team for seven years, Jets fans could never be sure.

"Walton has no personality. . . . The only emotion [he] evokes is disdain. Personality aside, Walton earned his low standing. He appears flustered by the intricacies of running an entire football team. . . . The only things worse than his playcalling and game strategy are his draft selections."
                                    —Paul Fichtenbaum, magazine writer

Actually, the one sure way that Jets fans could tell that Walton was alive and breathing was by his personal grooming habits on the sideline during a game:

"The football Jets are just going to have to do something about coach Joe Walton's picking his nose over NBC every Sunday on the sidelines during big games. If owner Leon Hess can't control Joe, perhaps [lineman] Marty Lyons could pinion both arms at crucial moments."
                                    —James Brady, *Advertising Age*

The writers were hard on old Joe, and so were the fans and players. During his years as coach the chant of "Joe must go! Joe must go!" was sung more often than the Star Spangled Banner at the Meadowlands. One disgruntled fan went so far as to hire a plane to fly over the stadium trailing a banner that read, "IF THIS PLANE HAD JOE WALTON'S BRAIN, IT WOULD BE FLYING BACKWARD."

In 1989, Walton's last year as coach, the criticism was unstinting. Greg Logan, a writer, attacked a Walton personnel decision as "a spineless move that is typical of his weak-kneed leadership over the past seven seasons." Joe Klecko, one of the Jets' all-time great players, said that Walton had taken over "a potential Super Bowl team and run it into the ground." And the *New York Post*

Jets fans chanted, "Joe must go! Joe must go!" And finally Joe went.

said it all with its headline about the Jets under Walton: "Green Slime."

One of Walton's major flaws as a head coach, besides the fact that he lost too many games, appeared to be in the area of player relationships. Klecko said that Walton once called the players a bunch of "pea brains who will never amount to anything after football." Then, after a horrible stomping at the hands of the

Colts, Walton gave the Jets a never-to-be-forgotten locker-room pep talk: "You guys are stealing money," he told his team.

Left for dead in New York, Walton resurfaced the next season as offensive coordinator for the Steelers where, after some initial problems, he was credited with helping to engineer a much improved, far more explosive Pittsburgh attack. See, from bum to genius in only a season!

The carcasses of onetime genius coaches turned bums are lying all over the NFL. Mike Shanahan, the offensive wizard of the Denver Broncos and the chief diaper changer for John Elway, was advertised as the man who would revive the long-dormant Raiders franchise. He was handed his hat four games into his second season as coach, and few in LA were sorry to see him go:

"I wasn't quite ready for the communist regime that came in. They wanted everyone wearing the same uniform, everyone doing the same thing and saying the same thing. The robot society was not in the Raiders' cards. . . . I hated to go to work for a year and a half."
—Howie Long, Raider defensive tackle

Another coach promoted from the assistant ranks is Wayne Fontes of Detroit. Like Shanahan and so many others, he has found that it's one thing to work behind the scenes and quite another to be the fellow whose decisions are dissected by millions of fire-breathing fans in the stadium and watching on TV. Fontes has brought life to Detroit, instituting the run 'n' shoot, but some people don't like the way he's handled pint-sized ground-gainer Barry Sanders:

"Benching Barry Sanders because he didn't block is like firing Picasso because he didn't wash his hands."
—Mitch Albom, Detroit sportswriter

A much sharper attack on Fontes was delivered by linebacker Jimmy Williams, who was benched during a game and then got into a verbal brawl with defensive coordinator Woody Widenhofer. The next day Williams was released, and he didn't like it at all. Said Williams:

"I don't know who coaches the defense. Woody coaches one moment, Lenny [Fontes, Wayne's brother] coaches one moment, Lamar [Leachman] coaches one moment. The worst thing Wayne did was hire his brother, because it doesn't allow Woody to coach.

The perception among players is that Lenny's the defensive coordinator and that Woody's a lame duck."

Then Williams lit into his former coach for having an Alaska-sized ego and drinking on plane flights:

"The worst thing that's happened to Wayne is he's become a head coach. He's lost touch with his players. He's caught up with himself and his glory. Every player on the team sees it. He's probably the most selfish person I've seen. He's a shadow of what he once was, which was a very, very good coach. It's the perfect example of how power and position can destroy a man. Wayne doesn't practice what he preaches. We're flying to and from games and he's drunk, flirting and kissing the stewardesses on the plane. And this is a commitment to winning? I believe we deserve better."

Fontes responded, "That's full of bleep. That is slanderous coming from him. That is not true. No one drinks on the plane."

Accusing your coach of being a drinker and pinching stewardesses is a somewhat novel twist, but attacking him as a lying, incompetent boob is routine procedure in the NFL these days, especially when the person doing the attacking has just been released from the team. How can Coach not be a dunderhead? He just cut me!

Retired players are another source of potential vindictiveness toward their former coaches. Witness Terry Bradshaw's broadsides against Pittsburgh icon Chuck Noll or Joe Theismann's cracks at Joe Gibbs. In widely publicized remarks, Theismann said that the field boss of the Redskins was "untouchable and unreachable," that his staff was full of "yes-men," and that he had "stolen the character of the team." Anything else, Joe?

Dexter Manley fits in the "Disgruntled Former Players" category. He, too, blasted Gibbs after the 'Skins decided not to keep Dexter following his drug suspension and rehabilitation. Picked up by Joe Bugel's Phoenix Cardinals late in the 1990 season, Manley showed his mouth was still in good working order after the long layoff:

"See, the Redskins have to justify letting me go, but they don't need to get personal. A lot of their coaches are zero coaches, if we're gonna get personal. Bugel [formerly with the Redskins] was a plus. Larry Peccatiello was a plus . . . but there are a lot of zeros on Gibbs's staff."

And while you're on the subject, Dexter, how would you rate your former coach against his peers?

"Red Miller, Art Shell, Buddy Ryan, Bum Phillips—people want to play for them. Same with Bugel . . . Joe Gibbs is not in that category. With Bugel, it's no Vietnam during practice. Gibbs, I hear, is kicking their butts in practice, which is fine when you're winning but not when you're getting your butts kicked in games."

If you've been around for a while, like Gibbs has, you've been a genius and a bum three or four times at least. You've learned to deal with the Manleys of this world—"The only thing you have to understand is that Manley has the IQ of a grapefruit," as Mike Ditka has said—and you just go on with the business of trying to win football games until the inevitable occurs and they ship you out in a pine box or you're fired, whichever comes first.

There's no question that the "genius" tag is overworked in football, especially when it comes to coaching. I mean, it's not exactly brain surgery now, is it?

"You draw Xs and Os on a blackboard and that's not so difficult. I can even do it with my left hand."
                    —John McKay, ex-football coach, on the so-called
                        "intellectualism" involved in coaching

But if there was one authentic coaching "genius"—and the term is used advisedly—in recent football history, it probably was Bill Walsh, late of the 49ers. He was so smart and forbidding, he was scary.

"Bill was like Darth Vader. You never knew what he was thinking. . . . He was always watching you. There was a definite dark side there."
                        —Harris Barton, 49er lineman

Starting from almost nothing, Walsh built the 49ers into one of the best pro teams ever, rivaled only by Chuck Noll's Steelers and Vince Lombardi's Green Bay Packers. What's more, he was as imaginative as most football coaches are stodgy, winning championships with his seemingly unstoppable short-passing attack as well as opening up the entire pro game.

Still, there were plenty of skeptics. After a Monday night game in which Walsh made a series of coaching errors, one writer scoffed at the coach's reputation as an intellect:

"If you had given the San Francisco coach a penny for his thoughts Monday night, he would have been overpaid."
—Brian Hanley, Chicago columnist

Terry Bradshaw was another who thought Walsh's reputation was overblown:

"You know, he believes that genius tag. . . . But the genius really wears No. 16 [Joe Montana]. That's the genius, and Walsh was messing with him. Walsh was trying to move him out, and now Walsh is out. Look who won."

Bradshaw was referring to a quarterback controversy that had plagued the 49ers since Walsh brought in Steve Young to replace Montana as quarterback. Young started some games, and there were rumors that Montana would be traded. But Joe stayed on, kept his position as the No. 1 man, and led the 49ers to back-to-back Super Bowl titles in 1989 and 1990, the second one coming after Walsh had left and George Siefert replaced him. Bradshaw, again:

"Walsh was wanting to bench [Montana] and play his other guy, Young, because if Young can go in there and do it, then Bill looks like another genius again."

It was not just Bradshaw who resented Walsh's image as a coaching genius; many of his players did too. Montana included, they wanted to show that Walsh was not the sole reason for the 49ers' success all those years.

"Bill made so many enemies. He was the type who had everything, but he could never enjoy it. He was a miserable human being."
—Keith Fahnhorst, 49er lineman

"When we lost to the Minnesota Vikings in the '87 playoffs, Walsh couldn't talk to us the day after. He lost a lot of respect with the players. When it was going well, he was there. When the ship was shaky, he couldn't face us."
—Eric Wright, 49er defensive back

Montana said that Walsh's leaving was "like driving down the highway and you roll down the window and you get a breath of fresh air." Bubba Paris said, "I felt like I lost about 200 pounds of genius off my back." And Ronnie Lott was bothered that Walsh didn't tell the team directly that he was retiring:

"I was extremely hurt that Bill didn't ever tell us as a team that he was retiring. He never said good-bye. It was unusual that Bill wasn't closer to us at the end."

Still, as every coach knows, you can't please everybody. And despite Ronnie Lott's hurt feelings, Walsh did show true genius in the end. He walked away at the top of the game, as coach of a Super Bowl champion.

3

Gangsters of Football: Jerry Glanville, Buddy Ryan and the University of Miami Hurricanes

Who is the most disliked coach in the NFL? Most people would probably say Jerry Glanville or Buddy Ryan. It's not hard to figure why. Both are blunt-spoken men whose teams play an outlaw brand of football. Both are also very good at what they do, which makes them even more irritating to their detractors.

"My coaching career is marred by two regrets. The first is that I never met George Halas or Vince Lombardi. My other regret is that I have met so many of the guys who are coaching now."

—Jerry Glanville

That's classic Glanville for you. Formerly with Houston, now with Atlanta, he's a man who revels in his image as the black-clad, motorcycle-riding, shoot-from-the-hip pariah of NFL football. In Glanville's world, you're either for 'im or agin' 'im. And you don't have to look far to find plenty of people who are agin' 'im.

"Glanville insists on violating the cardinal rule of the game with his mouth: Never give the other team incentive to beat you. He was gunned down here because of his cheap-shot mentality and his ego."

—Houston sports columnist, as quoted in *Esquire*

"I think he's an evil little toad. . . . He'll stab anybody in the back, that's my opinion. A lot of the players down there [Houston] don't like him. They've got so much talent Bozo the Clown could coach that team."

—Offensive lineman Harvey Salem, who played under Glanville at Houston before going to Detroit

Jerry Glanville in a typical pose: with his mouth open.

"I thank God that I did not have a chance to be coached by Jerry Glanville. I think . . . they have great talent in Houston. I never believed they had great coaching."
                              —Jim Everett, Rams quarterback

So what is it that people don't like about Jerry? For one, he seems to carry grudges to the grave. He makes enemies for life, and never forgets when someone burns him. Here, for instance, is what he had to say in reply to Jim Everett:

"He said he thanks God every day that he didn't have to play for us, that he was thankful to go somewhere where he could get good coaching. After we played against him twice, it was obvious he needed *great* coaching."

Or his opinion of the Houston sporting press, another of his enemies:

"I want to get them in the Astrodome in a ring, but they would arrest me for child abuse. They wouldn't get in a ring with me, anyway. They'd leak in their shoe."

And one more, for good measure:

"The difference between writers in Houston and writers in Atlanta is that in Atlanta some of the ones that can write can also read."

Glanville labored away in the assistant ranks for over a decade until Houston promoted him from defensive coordinator to head coach in 1985. The team he took over was one of the sorriest outfits to ever put on shoulder pads, as Glanville has noted on various occasions:

"When I got here in '84, we had the nicest guys in the NFL. Their mamas loved 'em. Their daddies loved 'em. But they wouldn't hit if you handed 'em sticks."

"The Oilers were a joke. Smack 'em in the mouth, pee on their pants, and they still wouldn't hit anybody."

"I've had sicker dogs and had them survive. That was an absolutely horrible team. Knute Rockne would have quit."

But Glanville did not quit, of course, gradually building the Oilers into a playoff-contending team while making a reputation for himself as the coach who would leave game tickets at Will-Call for celebrities both living (Ed McMahon, Loni Anderson) and dead (Elvis Presley, Buddy Holly, James Dean). The fans seemed to eat up his act, though Ernest Givens couldn't see it. "I don't know too many people who leave tickets for dead people," said the Oilers wide receiver. "That gets old."

Glanville's act did not stop at giving out tickets. On the sidelines he dresses only in black, wearing cowboy boots, long Johnny

Cash–style coats and belt buckles the size of frying pans. He made the Astrodome "the House of Pain" and turned those once cuddly Oilers into a bunch of brawling, bad-talking, finger-pointing street fighters.

"It's like professional wrestling down there. One day we're going to look on their sideline and see Hulk Hogan."

—Art Modell, Browns owner

If the Hulkster could play, Glanville would've hired him. He didn't care who played for him or what they did as long as they won. "We've got the Bengals this week. Are you scared?" he would say to his players to work them up for the game. "Are you going to wear high heels this week? You going to wear a skirt?"

Gradually, disillusionment set in. One Houston writer described Glanville as "a bozo in black" and said his coaching was "straight out of an LSD laboratory." The players came to agree. Warren Moon, the Oilers quarterback, said that Glanville—a defensive specialist—screwed up the offense by relying too much on his own instincts, his own hunches.

"Jerry's system was to let [his assistants] handle the concept, the game plan. He would let them do all the work during the week, and then on Sunday, Jerry would take over the play-calling. It was done by instinct! He would say, 'This series we're gonna open it up in a no-huddle and surprise 'em. Next series we're gonna punish 'em, run the lead draw right down the field. The next series we're gonna open it up again. You got me? You thinking with me?' O.K. Jerry."

Moon never got along with Glanville, who returned the favor by not once mentioning Moon's name in his book, only referring to him as "our quarterback." Moon was not the only Oiler who had trouble with the circus atmosphere that constantly surrounded the team and their coach, and many were glad to see him go. After Glanville described Atlanta's secondary as "real, not made out of paper or cardboard," like the one he had had in Houston, Oilers cornerback Patrick Allen laughed:

"That man's a joke. I didn't listen to him then, and I don't listen to him now."

John Davis, who played guard at Houston before moving on to the Bills, disliked Glanville's act intensely:

"The guy [Glanville] reaches a point where he wears on you with his B.S. He thinks it's funny and guys on the team are afraid to laugh at it. But it's just B.S. Always was, always will be. I don't even know why the guy bothers coaching. He's just wasting his time. All he wants to do is play up to people and be a celebrity. He ought to just go into some other field of entertainment."

But Glanville wasn't happy with a great many things in Houston as well, which he has made abundantly clear since leaving for the Falcons. He frequently had disputes with the septuagenarian general manager of the Oilers, Mike Holovak. Said Glanville:

"I don't know why we didn't get along. Most dead people like me."

Nor did Glanville like what he saw as Holovak's overly cautious player acquisitions:

"He won't take any chances. He likes draft choices better than sex."

In Glanville's first game as Atlanta coach, in 1990, the Falcons whipped the Oilers by 20 points. Afterward he was in rare form, making his famous "Texas can kiss my ass" comment as well as taking a potshot at the man who replaced him in Houston, Jack Pardee:

"Last year somebody ran up 99 points [actually 95] on SMU, but SMU won the very next week. That's why I gave the game ball to Forrest Gregg. Yeah, that jerk from the other team from Texas ran up 99 points."

Gregg was the coach of SMU, and "that jerk" was Pardee, then coaching for the University of Houston. Asked for his response, Pardee said:

"I might not have been called that [jerk] before, but I'm more embarrassed that we lost the game. I don't care what people say. He certainly knows what a jerk is. Some people's egos just can't be fed enough."

Glanville's post-game comments caused a sensation, particularly in Texas, and it helped remind the Oilers of how fortunate they were that Jerry was history:

Jack Pardee, "the jerk," replaced Glanville in Houston, and a whole bunch of Oilers were happy about it.

"It shows the kind of human being Jerry Glanville is. When I hear something like that, it makes me feel sorry for Glanville that he wasn't born a few inches taller so he wouldn't be so insecure."

—Steve Brown, Houston defensive back

Glanville was unrepentant, though, and even took another swipe at Pardee after that. "He must be a great coach," said

Glanville. "He's making three times as much as the last guy they had in there."

But this kind of thing is nothing new for Glanville. He's had dustups with a number of coaches, notably Chuck Noll. After a game in 1987 in which, as Mark Kram says, the Steelers were "all but put in body bags" by the ferocious Oiler defense, the Pittsburgh coach clamped onto Glanville's hand at midfield and wouldn't let it go. "You tried to hurt us," Noll said angrily. "Your guys coming over, jumping on people like that, you're going to get your ass in trouble." For this, and other slights, Glanville has developed an almost palpable hatred for Noll, and vice versa.

Here are a pair of Glanville comments on the four-time Super Bowl–winning coach:

"Can you imagine being the last man on earth with Chuck Noll? Lookin' at that face? I had a face injury once. The doctors wanted to cut. The trouble was I'd never smile again. Just like Chuck Noll."

"Chuck Noll was the most brutal coach in history. When he was on top, he had his players whip you like a hound. In the early eighties, they ground Warren Moon's head into the dirt, you needed a drill to get it out. When I took over, I made my men watch that film. I vowed Noll would never do it again. Now he just whines."

Cold, man. That's cold, Jerry. But wait, it gets better. The Glanville-Noll feud is kissy-face stuff compared to Glanville and Sam Wyche. Wyche, like Noll, believes that Glanville encourages unnecessary roughness and teaches such dirty tactics as spearing and hitting late. Said Wyche:

"That's the way they're coached and their coach brags about the fact they do this kind of thing. I guess there's an element of society that likes to break people's noses and another element that likes to conduct the sport within the rules of the game."

The enmity between the two coaches rubbed off on their players, and the Oilers-Bengals games a few years ago were little more than organized brawls in helmets and shoulder pads. In one game Oilers defensive back Chris Dishman decked Boomer Esiason and stood over him yelling, "You're in the House of Pain now, Boomer! It's all over!"

Esiason then bounced up and said, "Hey, Dishman, why don't

you go cover Eddie Brown one on one so we can get back in this game real quick?"

"They've got some players who are so bleeping arrogant. They feel that they are better fathers, uncles . . . that their wives are better than our wives, their organization is better, their colors look better. They just hate everything about us. If you've got somebody who hates you with cruel hatred, you've got to be quick, smart and just a little more wicked than they are."

—Sean Jones, Oilers defensive end, describing the
Oilers-Bengals rivalry

"I've never been around a team that could bring out the hatred in you like Houston. On the second series, [defensive end] William Fuller absolutely cheap-shotted me. He took three steps after I released the ball and earholed me, waxed me to the ground. . . . After that, we just wanted 'em."

—Boomer Esiason, Bengals quarterback

Esiason was describing an incident in one of the more infamous games in recent NFL history—Cincinnati's 61–7 shellacking of the Oilers during the 1989 season. This was pure revenge for the Bengals and Sam Wyche. They wanted blood, and Wyche admitted as much in the locker room following the rout:

"I wish this had been a five-quarter game. We would have loved to have jumped into that triple-digit thing. We don't like this team. We don't like their people. It couldn't happen to a nicer team. . . . After their players and their coach did all that talking, they got embarrassed and humiliated today. We were going for the jugular."

No kidding. Leading 45–0, the Bengals tried an onside kick and recovered it. With 21 seconds remaining, they kicked a field goal to rub still more salt in the wound. Tell us about it, Sam:

"Any time teams are mouthy, constantly running their mouth, somewhere along the line someone is going to put it together and they're going to be annihilated. If you're the Houston Oilers, you'd better expect it. They just got what they deserved, and maybe not enough of it. . . . It's the dumbest, most undisciplined, stupid football team I think we've ever played. You can only be so stupid, but the Oilers have exceeded the limits. They're a team with no discipline, and when you have no discipline you have no chance of winning."

Just in case his message wasn't clear, Wyche called Glanville "a liar" and "the biggest phony in professional football," adding:

"Jerry is an unusual coach. He really is an unusual coach. Drop me a note if you find somebody who likes this guy, will you?"

Okay, Sam, we will. In the meantime we'll move on to another controversial member of the coaching fraternity, Buddy Ryan. Ryan and Glanville have a lot in common. Both were assistants for many years until they got their big shot at head coaching. Both are defensive wizards. Both inspire tremendous loyalty from their staff and players (at least initially), even as the aggressive, in-your-face brand of football they teach creates enemies on the other side of the ball.

"I thought Houston was dirty. Hey, Jerry Glanville's boys look like a church choir compared to these guys [the Eagles]. They did flat-out dirty things. Once that included grabbing below the belt. They're cheap, cheap women."

—Cards fullback Ron Wolfley,
after a game against Ryan's Eagles

"I don't agree with the way Buddy does things. He tries to talk junk about the other players and shows no class. I hate a person like that. Why can't he just be a professional, do his job and let the game be played?"

—David Archer, Falcons quarterback

Buddy came to fame, of course, as the man who helped construct perhaps the best defensive team in football history, the 1986 Chicago Bears. The Bears pulverized the Broncos in the Super Bowl, and Ryan received wide credit for masterminding their vaunted "46" defense. But he frequently quarreled with head coach Mike Ditka, another man of strong opinions, and denigrated Ditka's role in the success of the Bears. Late in 1984 Buddy was inspecting his bonus check in the company of some players after Chicago had beaten Washington in a playoff game. "Not bad for saving the asshole's job," said Ryan, referring to Ditka.

Ryan has also commented on Ditka's participation in the Bears' drafting procedures:

"Ditka spends the off-season playing golf, then shows up in the draft room and looks busy. I never thought he was too strong in personnel. He never could evaluate talent when I was there."

Ryan (like Jerry Glanville or Ditka himself) is not afraid to lead with his mouth. He is, as Leigh Montville has noted, "the NFL's master of bombast, invective and general all-around bluster." Again like Glanville, he puts down opponents and even players on his own team. When he was with the Bears he referred to Refrigerator Perry as "that wasted draft pick" and said that defensive tackle Jerome Brown's problem was "brains."

When he went over to the Eagles Buddy remained true to himself, referring to the team he inherited as "trash." Said Ryan: "We had guys who couldn't play dead playing quarterback." After watching running back Earnest Jackson perform poorly in practice, he told one of his assistants, "Get him out of here. Trade him for a six-pack of beer—and it doesn't even have to be cold." Once he was asked if he had lost confidence in wide receiver Henry Williams. "I never had any confidence in him to begin with," replied Ryan.

Ryan's lack of diplomatic aplomb extended as well to the team's ownership. He referred to Eagles owner Norman Braman, who has a summer home overseas, as "the guy in France." And he described Harry Gamble, the Eagles president, as Braman's "illegitimate son." But Ryan's biggest crime, in the eyes of management, was that he openly sided with the players in their 1987 labor dispute with the owners. Coaches were supposed to support their bosses, or at least stay quiet about it if they didn't. Many in the NFL establishment did not like Ryan's undisguised contempt for the replacement teams who played during the lock-out.

"In addition to being a football coach, he [Ryan] has certain responsibilities to the league. And certain things he has said and done are not beneficial to the league."
—Tex Schramm, Cowboys general manager

But what did Buddy care if some of the things he said weren't beneficial to the league? Some of the things he said weren't beneficial to his own team, and that never seemed to bother him. Ryan seemed to take great delight in mocking the opposition whenever the opportunity arose. After playing (and whipping) the Dolphins in an exhibition game, Ryan crowed,

"I wish we played the Dolphins twice a year, because you want to have as many patsies on your schedule as possible."

After picking up free-agent linebacker Paul Butcher from the Lions and then watching him throw up in his first practice with the Eagles, Ryan commented,

"Yeah, he threw up four or five times. I should've known better than to take anybody out of Detroit. They're not in shape. They think 8–8 is a good season."

On defensive coach Bud Carson, Buddy has said, "I can remember when he fucked up a pretty good defense in Kansas City," and then there is his classic comment on how his defense was going to stop the running and scrambling of a young Joe Montana: "It's hard to throw running on your butt, you know."

It hardly needs be said that Ryan's bluster and bombast—as well as all the brash talking by his Eagle players—did not go over so well with those on the receiving end of it. Mike Ditka got sweet revenge after his Bears trounced the Eagles in a much ballyhooed 1989 game. Said Ditka:

"We're not the best, but we know they're not the best. They think they can come in here and talk their way into a game. They got that from their coach, the fat man."

In the playoffs that season, all the Eagles could talk about was how much they wanted to face the 49ers in the NFC finals. Unfortunately, though, they still had to play the Rams, who then proceeded to knock them on their keisters and out of the playoffs.

"I think we turned out the lights on all the talkers. We would love to get a chance of playing the 49ers, but we're not going to talk about it. We just witnessed stupidity and we're not going to copy it."

—John Robinson, Rams head coach

Before the Rams game, Ryan had mocked LA's "junior high school defense." One Rams player referred to this when he said,

"Sometimes junior high defenses are tough, especially when you're playing elementary school guys."

Ryan's caustic style—and the brutally physical play of his charges—came back to haunt the Eagles again and again, especially during playoff time. During the 1990 season the Eagles pounded the Redskins, roughing up a number of Washington players. Plagued by injuries even before the game, the Redskins were forced to start journeyman quarterback Jeff Rutledge in place of injured starter Mark Rypien. After the game Ryan heaped scorn on Rutledge: "He's an old quarterback—he's been around 100 years. We just thought we could get to him."

The Redskins did not forget this game, and when they met Philadelphia again in the first round of the playoffs, it was the Eagles that got pounded this time. On the sidelines Ryan seemed helpless and confused. On top of that he humiliated Randall Cunningham, his star quarterback, by pulling him out for a series of plays in the second half and replacing him with the washed-up second-stringer Jim McMahon, a bizarre move that ultimately led to his firing and caused much snickering in the media.

"What do you imagine was whistling through Buddy's empty noggin—besides the wind—when he had the brainstorm to pull Cunningham? What flavor Ultra Slim-Fast milk shake is he drinking, Mr. Coconut Head?"

—Tony Kornheiser, columnist

"The Eagles should have fired Buddy Ryan, and announced the location of his car, as soon as the final seconds ticked off. He deserves worse. I'm sure everyone was thinking that Jim McMahon could spark the Eagles. Sure, Buddy, bite on a few more lemons and maybe your brain will completely dry up."

—Steve Tady, sportswriter

Some of the Eagles, including Cunningham, reacted with shock and dismay at Ryan's firing, but a few others privately expressed relief. As an unidentified Eagle once said,

"Mixed emotions is watching your new car fly off a cliff with Buddy Ryan in it."

It may not be fair to lump a college team—the University of Miami—in with a pair of pro coaches like Glanville and Ryan, but then again, it wasn't exactly fair what the Hurricanes did to Texas at the Cotton Bowl now, was it? On New Year's Day 1991, Miami stomped the Longhorns 46-3 in a virtuoso display of gangster football. They taunted, they danced, and they received no fewer than nine penalties for unsportsmanlike conduct.

"If we learned nothing else Tuesday, it was that Miami, despite two losses, has the team most likely to win a football game on any given day that the majority of the players can make bail."

—Mike Littwin, columnist

There's nothing surprising about Miami's conduct in the Texas game. They've been behaving like a bunch of reform school dropouts for years, practically ever since they came onto the national scene as a college football power.

"You've heard of Pop Art? Miami has perfected Pop-off Art. The Hurricane players yell insults and scream derision. They waggle a finger in your face like some arrogant probation officer. They follow even the most prosaic tackle with pelvic grinds and bumps that would be disgraceful if they weren't so laughable."

—Art Spander, columnist

The university says it has made an effort to crack down on the thuggery and thinks that things will improve now that the biggest offenders—"the last renegade class," as one senior put it—have played their final game at the Cotton Bowl.

Still, as the examples of Buddy Ryan and Jerry Glanville vividly attest, the character of a football team largely derives from its coach, so it's up to Hurricane coach Dennis Erickson to finally put an end to the nonsense.

"The Miami Hurricanes, good as they are, are the Wrestlemania of college football. And it's a little late in the game, frankly, for Coach Dennis Erickson to say how choked up he is about his players' behavior. A coach sets a tone about all that, same as he sets a tone about going to class and about cheating and all the rest of it. Compared with Miami's football players, Jerry Tarkanian's Runnin' Rebels are the Harvard-Yale game."

—Mike Lupica, columnist

4

They Call Them Assassins: The Cheap-Shot Artists of the NFL

Cheap shots are as much a part of the game of football as bosomy cheerleaders bouncing on the sidelines and marching bands at halftime. As evil and nasty as they are, they remain a brutally effective, time-tested method of punishing and intimidating an opponent.

The most notorious of the modern-day cheap-shot artists is Andre "Dirty" Waters, the Eagles safety who has been fingered as "the NFL's dirtiest player" by *The National* sports daily and a number of others:

"Andre Waters is the cheap-shot artist of the NFL. . . . This is a guy who goes after people with the intention of hurting them."
—Dan Dierdorf, *Monday Night Football*

"I've seen him end a guy's career. I've seen him come after me and I've seen him go after a lot of other guys. He's the worst."
—Jim Everett, Rams quarterback

Waters once took a swipe at Everett's knee and is said to have ended Steve Bartkowski's career with a shot to his knees. Minnesota quarterback Rich Gannon called Waters "a cheap-shot artist" after he dove in after Gannon's knees in a game. Again, Everett on unclean Andre:

"The man has problems. He's a very aggressive ballplayer, no doubt. But there's a fine line between being an aggressive ballplayer and being a [expletive]."

Waters denies being a cheap-shotter, but if he's guilty, he's certainly not alone. Another of the players singled out by *The National* as a cheap-shot specialist was offensive lineman Ron Heller, a teammate of Waters's on the Eagles.

"He's a sucker puncher, leg-whipper, a modern-day Conrad Dobler who can't play."

—NFL coach, as quoted in *The National*

"[The media] came up to me before the game and asked me about Heller being a cheap player and I couldn't see anything that illustrated that on film. But after I played against the guy in the first quarter, it was ridiculous."

—Bruce Smith, Buffalo defensive end

Until he was fired, the coach of Waters and Heller was Buddy Ryan. Former Oilers safety Jeff Donaldson learned his football under Jerry Glanville. Says a former Glanville assistant about Donaldson:

"If you play for Glanville, you're dirty. Jerry taught him everything they both know."

It's a total distortion, however, to say that Glanville and Ryan are the only coaches who allow dirty football on their teams. A number of players play dirty on teams all around the league, despite the phony lip service that other coaches give to staying "within the rules." If a coach has a team that's winning games, if he can get away with it, he'll look the other way when one of his players earholes somebody.

In another game, Bruce Smith accused Jets tight end Mark Boyer of playing dirty, nearly coming to blows with him outside their locker rooms. Said an enraged Smith to Boyer,

"That's my career, man. You keep doing it and I'll get you. If not on the field, I'll get you off."

Kansas City defensive end Neil Smith put a late hit on Broncos quarterback John Elway, prompting Elway to issue a warning to Smith after the game:

"He cold-cocked me from the back side. I just told him I thought it was a cheap shot. I told him this year is over but we get to see them twice next year and I'm looking forward to it."

The 49ers have been repeatedly criticized for their offensive-line blocking techniques, specifically "the chop block" aimed at the lower legs and ankles.

"They take more cheap shots than any offensive line I've seen in my nine years in the league. I think it's something they teach.

They let you go up the field a little, then go for your knees. It should be outlawed."
> —Donnell Thompson, Colts defensive lineman

"They cut me on the back of the knees. They could have ended my career. I don't think what they did was fair."
> —Harvey Armstrong, a linemate of
> Thompson's on the Colts

Chuck Thomas, a backup center for the 49ers, said the Colt linemen were "crybabies," but other players on other teams have said similar things about San Francisco and the techniques taught by their offensive-line coach, Bob McKittrick. After a game against the 49ers, Raiders defensive tackle Howie Long chased McKittrick down and shouted at him, "I wish I were in uniform so I could kick your ass!" Later Long added,

"You only wish McKittrick was 50 pounds heavier and 20 years younger. So you wouldn't feel bad about kicking his ass."

McKittrick, an ex-Marine now in his fifties, responded:

"I was going to congratulate Howie, but I changed my mind. He's somewhat of a bully. He doesn't lose well."

One of the most egregious examples of San Francisco's blocking tactics came early in the 1990 Super Bowl when Denver's defensive star Karl Mecklenburg had to leave the game after being leg-whipped by 49er offensive guard Bruce Collie. Mecklenburg suffered a hyperextended knee and heaped ridicule on the man who did it to him: "I guess he doesn't have the talent to block you any other way."

McKittrick, the guru for Collie (who's since left the 49ers) and Bubba Paris, another notorious cut-blocker, claimed his team's hands were clean:

"It's all legal as long as it's not from the back side. He [Mecklenburg] can be mad for as long as he plays. He doesn't have much to be proud of, like the rest of their defense."

Lawrence Taylor of the Giants had to be carted off the field in a 1989 game with the 49ers. Lying on his back as he was being taken away, he shouted, "Get Walls," referring to 49er tight end Wesley Walls, who had hit Taylor away from the play and caused a hairline fracture of his right foot. Taylor later backed down from a vow of revenge against Walls, but his teammates were not so sure. "It was a blatant cheap shot," said Leonard Marshall. "It was not necessary," added Pepper Johnson. "Lawrence was no factor in the play whatsoever. . . . It kind of ticks you off."

One of the most vocal critics of the 49ers is David Fulcher, the Bengals defensive back who after a game with San Francisco accused a number of men in red and gold of hitting late, particularly blocking tight end Jamie Williams. Said Fulcher:

"When the play is over, this guy [Williams] was out there punching me in the back, holding me and stepping on my feet. It's the stuff that's really stupid. These guys do things that people don't see as far as punching and trying to stick you in the eye. They're cheap-shot artists. I'm assuming people are looking past all their cheap shots because of how good they are."

Fulcher's anger swelled to include the entire 49er team and its arrogant "Team of the Decade" attitude:

"I hate a team like that. I wish we could have San Francisco on our schedule 16 times a year because I want to play them again. We're a little ticked because people put that team on a pedestal and we're tired of hearing about it. This was like a rich high school playing a poor high school. We don't have any banners; they do."

The 49ers of course defended themselves against Fulcher's attack:

"If you go back on the films and look to see who was doing the most cheap shotting, I think you would find out that they were doing a heck of a lot more than we were."
—Harry Sydney, 49ers fullback

"You look at the film and see how many plays David Fulcher made, then tell me what grounds he has to say we play dirty. The guy is nonexistent. I hate to see a guy do that. That's crying. It's a physical game. If he didn't want any part of it he should have stayed on injured reserve."
—Jamie Williams

On the other side of the ball, the 49ers defense has also been involved in some late-hit disputes. Asked about a reported comment that he was going to try to "damage" John Elway in the Super Bowl, linebacker Charles Haley denied ever making such a remark, explaining:

"I didn't say nothing about damage. What I said was we're going to hit Elway, and if it costs 15 yards, it costs 15 yards. That ain't saying nothing about damaging him."

Thank you for that clarification, Charles. Haley was thrown out of a game against the Rams after bumping the referee in protest of a personal foul penalty called against him for a late hit on Jim Everett. Said Haley the next day:

"If I would have known I was going to get kicked out of the game, I would have tried to cripple the SOB."

Even Ronnie Lott, the widely admired defensive mainstay of all those 49er Super Bowl teams, got into a shoving and name-calling match with Atlanta receiver Shawn Collins. Collins told his version of events this way:

"I don't appreciate the kind of player Lott is. I don't appreciate the way he sticks you after every play. He's a dirty player, a headhunter. Even when they had the game in the bag, he was still after me. I was beatin' him all day. I guess he doesn't like a rookie beatin' him like that. I heard him tell Bobby Butler [Atlanta cornerback] that I'm on his list now, that he's gonna get me."

When told of Collins's remarks in the locker room after the game, Lott, normally a placid fellow off the field, exploded:

"Hey, no one pushes me off when I make a tackle. You tell him I'm lookin' for him. Tell him I'll be head-huntin' him for the rest of my career."

Collins and Lott later kissed and made up, which is one reason why one of the greatest cheap-shot artists of all time, Conrad "The Meanest Man in Football" Dobler, thinks today's NFL players are a bunch of girl scouts. "These guys play like it's a day at the office," he says. "It's antiseptic. Hey, if you want sophistication, go to a tennis match." For instance, says Dobler, look at a guy like Mike Singletary of the Bears:

"He's not a mean guy. He helps people up, man. Hey, you mow them down for three hours and spit on the guy."

Dobler belongs to an older generation of football players who played as mean and dirty as the meanest and dirtiest of today's cheap-shot artists. Maybe even more so, in fact.

When Ronnie Lott says, "Hey, no one pushes me off when I make a tackle," you believe him.

"We glamorize hoodlums. The guys who foul and hold. The worst examples of sportsmanship become our heroes. The way Conrad Dobler plays is nothing to emulate."
                    —Darryl Royal, University of Texas coach

Dobler wrote a book boasting about his exploits as a rogue elephant of football. It sold lots of copies. Another famous author and hit man is Jack Tatum, whose devastating hit on Patriots receiver Darryl Stingley in a 1978 exhibition game left him paralyzed for life. It was a legal tackle, but nevertheless one of the most vicious acts of violence ever seen in organized sports.

Tatum, whose nickname was "Black Death," first got his reputation as a big hitter at Ohio State. In those days the best collegiate players met the NFL champion in a pre-season contest known as the "College All Star Game." When Tatum played in the game, fresh out of college, he faced the Baltimore Colts of Johnny Unitas and John Mackey. Mackey, one of the best tight ends ever, caught a pass early in the game and was tackled by Tatum, who couldn't get a clean shot at his target and only made a feeble take-down. "Hard-hitting rookie . . . What a joke!" said Mackey as he jogged back to the huddle laughing.

The Black Death got his revenge later in the game. After catching a pass Mackey was leveled by Tatum, who this time had a clear, unobstructed approach. His helmet into the ribs dropped Mackey instantly and left him gasping for air on the ground. Standing over him, Tatum smiled, "How's that for a joke?"

After Tatum joined the Raiders he helped form one of the hardest-hitting secondaries that ever played, a group that included the equally notorious George Atkinson. Atkinson is remembered primarily as the man who knocked Pittsburgh's Lynn Swann out of a game with an extraordinarily fierce forearm shot to the head. The forearm swat occurred away from the play, and gave Swann a concussion. In a famous remark, Steelers head coach Chuck Noll saw Atkinson's hit as a blatant act of criminality.

"You have a criminal element in all aspects of society. Apparently we have it in the NFL too. Maybe we have a law and order problem."

Others joined in the condemnation:

"There was nothing brave or daring about it. A tough guy looks you in the eye, plays you jaw to jaw. It's a tough game. But that wasn't tough, and it wasn't football."
—Darryl Royal

"It was a real bad cheap shot. He should have been thrown out of the game. It was the most flagrant cheap shot I've seen all year."
—Sammie White, Vikings receiver

In a classic bit of damage control, Al Davis, the owner of the Raiders, defended Atkinson's right to maim and injure and accused the media of blowing the incident out of proportion. Said Davis:

"No one was killed. Why get excited? You wrote as though the Pittsburgh game was the My Lai massacre. You guys are the problem. You want us to win. You want us to be tough. But when we're in a vicious game with the Steelers, a team that is notorious for busting up opponents, you seize on an incident involving one of our men and you hammer away."

The specific technique employed by Atkinson and used to nearly decapitate Swann was known around the league as "the George Atkinson Special." One player at the time explained how to do it: "That's where you stiffen the forearm and cock it back and hit the guy upside the head." But again, it would be a misrepresentation to portray Atkinson or Tatum as the focus of all evil in the football world when they played. Lots of folks were spearing and earholing and doing the Atkinson Special to their fellow man.

"The rules state that when a player is hit above the shoulders, there's supposed to be a penalty. Hell, there's Williams, sitting there with blood pouring out of his mouth. Did they think he bit himself?"
> —Tampa Bay coach John McKay, after Rams
> linebacker Jim Youngblood broke the jaw of Bucs
> QB Doug Williams by spearing him in the face mask

"This kid, Doug Plank of the Bears? His head comes flying in there with reckless abandon. It's awful."
> —Notre Dame coach Ara Parseghian,
> observing the pros

"I told Jones that I thought what he did was the cheapest thing I've ever seen. . . . I hope he gets his neck broken."
> —Steelers linebacker Jack Lambert, after seeing his
> teammate, Terry Bradshaw, picked up and
> driven headfirst into the ground by
> Cleveland defensive end Joe Jones

After the attacks on Bradshaw and others, the NFL put restrictions on the kinds of things that pass rushers could do to quarterbacks. But Lambert himself, who was so worried about his own quarterback's health, scoffed at the new rules. "Might as

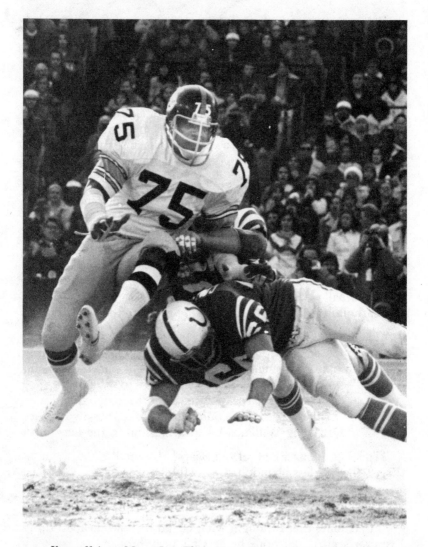

You tell 'em, Mean Joe: This ain't no game for quiche-eaters.

well put 'em in skirts," he said. No matter what the rules are, cheap shots—at the quarterback or anybody else—will never be eliminated because of the violence inherent in the game itself. And let's be honest with ourselves. What kind of game would it be anyway without all that leg-snapping, bone-cracking, head-hunting fun?

"You take violence out of the game, you'll lose a lot of fans. They can go to a baseball game if they don't want to see violence. I go for three innings, then I can't stand it and I'm out."

—Dennis Franks, Eagles safety

"People don't like to get hit, they should go play basketball. If people are going to cry about getting hit, they shouldn't put on shoulder pads and helmets. They should go play baseball. I hear you can make a lot of money playing baseball."

—Andre "Dirty" Waters

Or, in the immortal words of Mean Joe Greene:

"This ain't a game for pussies."

5

Free Spirits, or Just Plain Loudmouths? The Brash-Talkin', Trash-Talkin' Pop-Offs of Football

Football is a team game that demands uniformity. And conformity, to some extent. That's why someone like, oh, Eric Dickerson rubs so many people wrong. He won't conform. Plus, he's got a big mouth.

"Eric Dickerson is one of the most overrated players in the history of the sport."
—Pete Axthelm, football analyst

Dickerson, one of the biggest pop-offs in football, once called the vice-president of the Rams "an eel." He commented that Jim Irsay of the Indianapolis Colts, his current employer, "deserves to be a general manager as much as Daffy Duck does." He distrusts the media, whines constantly about money, complains ad nauseam about the violence of the game, and alienates his teammates with remarks about how crappy they are. The Colts, said Eric, "couldn't beat some of the worst Canadian league teams."

One of Eric's favorite riffs—one columnist dubbed him "The Sultan of Sulk"—involves his offensive line and what a rotten job they do blocking for him. Here are a few classic Dickersonisms on the subject:

"When my mother, who is 85 years old and watches football, says, 'These guys aren't blocking,' you know they're not doing the job."

"I'm not Superman, and if I was, right now I would have some kryptonite linemen in front of me. It's pitiful. We need some guys who can play. It's as simple as that. If we get that rectified, we'll have a really good football team. If we don't, I think we'll be terrible."

"[Playing for the Colts] is like taking a revolver and putting a bullet in it and spinning it and sticking it to my head, and sooner or later the trigger is going to come out and kill me, and that's the chance I'm taking."

You'd think Eric would lay off his offensive-line teammates, considering what power they hold over him and his pigskin-toting livelihood. "Hey, Butch, you read what Dickerson said about us in the papers yesterday?" "Yeah, Chuck, I saw it." "You thinking what I'm thinking?" "Yeah, Chuck." And then Butch and Chuck just happen to miss their blocks the next time Dickerson's number is called and SPLAT! there goes Eric.

Dickerson's bad boy image stems, in part, from the contract hassles he's had over the years with the Rams and Colts. Eric wants more money. The teams balk. Eric starts whining. Things deteriorate, and the next thing you know Eric is lying awake at night thinking of nasty things he can say to the press the next morning in order to force a trade. It happened with the Rams. First he said how he thought Georgia Frontiere ought to loosen up her purse strings:

"I think that as an organization they aren't committed to winning. They want to win, but they want to win it the cheap way. You can't do that."

And then he bitched about John Robinson's salary as coach:

"John makes more than all of us. All of the players, me too. He makes more than me. Let him run 47 Gap."

Dickerson's wish was eventually granted and he left the Rams in 1987, moving cross country to Indianapolis, where he got into more money squabbles despite being one of the highest-paid running backs in the league. The greatest running back to ever come out of Southern Methodist University wanted more moolah, though, and staged a holdout at the start of the '90 season. Pete Axthelm said he could understand Eric's demands—after all, "he just wants to make as much money as he did at SMU"—but others were not so forgiving.

One national reporter described him as "mercenary," and some people in Indianapolis—picking up on a trick from LA, where fans threw Monopoly money at Eric from the stands—had fun with a game similar to "Pin the Tail on the Donkey." Instead of a tail, they used a big wallet, and instead of a donkey there was a picture of our friend. It was called "Pin the Wallet on Eric."

During the holdout the Colts' brass said they were trying to move Dickerson, but couldn't find any takers around the league.

"I know no other team wants him. We told them to just make us an offer. Nobody did. Who wants a 30-year-old running back who can't play for John Robinson or his college coach, can be a malcontent and no money is good enough? Do you want your franchise subjected to that and give up draft choices and pay him a million and a half dollars?"

—Ron Meyer, Indianapolis coach

Well, as it turned out, the Colts did. They paid Dickerson a whole bunch of loot that will make him a wealthy man though probably not any happier. But at least it shut him up for a while.

Not that I'm against football players speaking their minds. Some of the hard-core gridiron types think that players should be seen not heard, but that would make for a pretty dull game. That's robot-ball, not football. Football should have room for the Jim McMahons and Neon Deions and Tim McKyers and Brian Bosworths, as obnoxious as they can be sometimes.

All right.

Forget the Boz.

Forget I ever said him. Was he a bad odor or what?

"I don't know how good he is, but I do know that he sure as hell gets run over a lot. He's got a gimmick, though, and everybody loves it. They're paying to see his hair. Maybe he's in the wrong business."

—Art Donovan, on the Boz before he found a new business besides football

Bosworth, in fact, was not a football player, he was a marketing concept. Fred Smerlas called him "a glorified safety with painted hair." He had freaky hair and sold antiperspirant on TV. Said columnist Scott Ostler: "He is the only football player in history to make more deodorant commercials than tackles."

As part of its promotional campaign with Bosworth, Gillette one year sent samples of Right Guard to each of the players whom Seattle was going to play next. "You're going to need this for all you will sweat trying to handle the Boz," an attached note said. Atlanta nose tackle Tony Casillas agreed that the Falcons did need some deodorant after playing against the Boz. "We're going to need it because he stunk up the place," said Casillas.

Asked how the Boz would fit in with the Bears, Dan Hampton said, "We'd make him dress in the basement." But if the Boz had one thing, it was nerve. As a rookie he criticized the Raiders for a lack of intensity, a charge that drew a rebuke from Sean Jones, a Los Angeles lineman:

"He hasn't been in the league long enough to know what intensity is. He's just a rookie, and he should get respect from the people in the league who know what the NFL is about, and stop worrying about haircuts."

The Boz never did get respect and apparently never did stop worrying about his hair, because he's now off in Hollywood trying to become the next Chuck Norris or Arnold Schwarzenegger and thankfully we don't have him to kick around anymore.

A guy who kind of reminds you of Bosworth is Tony Mandarich, another self-promoting head case who has so far been a big disappointment for the Packers. The Pack was fooled enough by Mandarich's heavy-lifting, Mr. Universe body to spend a No. 1 draft choice on him, and Tony returned the favor with a crack at the town where he was coming to play. About the only endorsements he'd ever get in Green Bay, he said after being drafted, would be selling snowmobiles.

"I'm being honest. Green Bay is not a metropolis. It's not Los Angeles or New York. It's not even Buffalo."

It may or may not say something about Tony that he evaluates cities on the basis of how many possible commercial endorsements he can pick up in them. There are many in the game, however, who think that Mandarich should worry a little less about his off-the-field endorsement portfolio and pay more attention to football.

"Oh, you mean Bozo? Bozo ought to stick to football, he doesn't have an acting career."
                    —Bears coach Mike Ditka, asked to comment on a
                        Mandarich television commercial

"I can't believe how Reggie was throwing Mandarich around. It was amazing. They are basically the same size, and Reggie treated him like a toy. I started to rush, and I had to watch to keep from tripping over him."
> —Eagles defensive tackle Mike Golic, after watching teammate Reggie White handle Mandarich in a game

"He's a joke. Tony doesn't play hardly at all and when he gets in, he doesn't do anything. He doesn't work out hard and he doesn't study films much. I think he could be a decent player if he worked at it, but he's not going to be the great player people think, not even close."
> —An NFL player, as quoted in the *San Francisco Chronicle,* during Mandarich's rookie season

We're afraid that that's probably true. Mandarich has a great future—only it's at Venice Beach pumping iron in his bikini shorts, not in the NFL. And when they write his playing obituary they'll say that his greatest flaw as a lineman was not that he talked a big game, but that he couldn't back it up. That's the pop-off's No. 1 rule: If you talk trash, you better be able to put the muscle behind it.

The jury is still out on Neon Deion Sanders, who would seem to be a perfect fit with the Jerry Glanville–led Atlanta Falcons. Glanville is a big talker, and so's his motormouth cornerback. "Boy, you keep runnin' that sloppy stuff, you goin' to Arena Football," he would tell opposing receivers when he was playing for Florida State, just before he'd predict how he was going to run a punt back for a touchdown and then do it. His antics enraged many—"If I see him in the pros, I'll probably kill him," said Florida receiver Ricky Nattiel, now with the Broncos—and drew wide publicity, which Prime Time has never shied from.

In the pros, however, Prime Time's routine has not gone over so well. The velvet-tongued Lester Hayes said his stardom in college came from "chasing down Caucasian Clydesdales" and that "his destiny is to spend some time in the penitentiary." Eagles coach Buddy Ryan called him "a coward" and said he "ought to be in track" rather than football. Similar opinions have been voiced elsewhere around the league.

"The Falcons have some defensive backs who wouldn't tackle my mom. And Deion Sanders just runs away from hitting people."
> —Bruce Collie, offensive lineman

Before a game with the Falcons in 1990, Bears defensive back Lemuel Stinson described Prime Time as "a nobody" who had no stomach for the hard business of hitting and tackling, saying:

"You never see [Sanders] putting his headgear down in there. He is not a cover guy, either. He can't cover our receivers man-to-man."

Then, during the game on Sunday, Neon retaliated for these remarks with a cheap shot against Stinson during an onside kick attempt. Or so said Stinson anyway:

"He [Sanders] has no class at all. They caught the ball a little early, and he hit me from the back. I tried to get up, and he was holding my face down, talking about how he was going to get some. He's just an ignorant guy. All the money he makes, he should have class. But if money makes you act like that, then I don't think I want to have that much money."

Prime Time denied the cheap-shot charge and in turn accused his accuser of lying about the incident:

"I'm just hurting from him lying about a lot of things. You can call Deion Sanders cocky, you can call him flamboyant, you can call him what you want to. But no one has ever called him a liar. My word is good, and [Stinson] is a liar."

A guy like Neon Deion gets it from all sides, and not just from people in football. Chet Fuller, an editorial writer for the *Atlanta Constitution,* attacked Sanders for being an inappropriate role model for young people.

"[He is] the latest in a disappointingly long line of hype-mongering sports stars . . . [who] sickeningly glorify the flashy, quick-success, easy-money lifestyle . . . cheating thousands of young kids who hang on their every word and can't wait for the day when they, too, sign the multimillion dollar contract and have their chests gold-plated."

It should be pointed out that Sanders does have friends and supporters, one of whom is Andre Rison, a teammate on the Falcons. After hearing what Lemuel Stinson was saying about his buddy before that Bears game, Rison engaged in some taunting of his own, claiming that Chicago had "some of the sorriest wide receivers in the league." Then he went after Stinson:

"If it's just me and him, we'll call 38 pass plays, I'll score 38 touchdowns. . . . If he plays me man-to-man the whole game, I'll be in the Hall of Fame by Monday. I've got my speech ready."

In the game itself, the Bears beat the Falcons 30–24. In the game within the game, Sanders had no impact, Rison caught six balls, and Stinson had two interceptions. "They came, they saw, we kicked their ass," said a triumphant Stinson, ending the debate, although it is likely neither Prime Time nor his friend Showtime (Rison's nickname) shall soon forget.

Tim McKyer of the Dolphins is another talented athlete whose propensity to speak his mind at inopportune moments has irritated not only his opponents, but his teammates as well. Before a 1990 playoff game against the Chiefs, McKyer said the Kansas City secondary was "suspect" and that his Dolphins would easily handle them. Dan Marino and Don Shula were among those who told him to shut his face, but that's something McKyer apparently has a hard time doing.

"McKyer's best offensive weapon—and his most offensive— always has been his mouth. If a reporter needed a quote, well, there was Tim circulating around the locker room, panting for attention. Rarely has an athlete needed so desperately to see his name in the newspapers."

—Lowell Cohn, *San Francisco Chronicle*

McKyer wore out his welcome in San Francisco—as he did in Miami—because he couldn't seem to fit in with the team system. He chose the week before San Francisco's Super Bowl game with the Broncos to declare his independence:

"The 49ers have always wanted me to be grateful, but I wanted to be paid. I don't buy this . . . about the 49ers system. I'm not a company guy going to give you a company line. I have a problem being in a system where you're not appreciated and it's like you're swept under the rug and they want you to wear a muzzle. I know my importance to this ball club and my value, and they want to act like I don't exist. I'm not a troublemaker. I'm just right."

The 49ers didn't see it this way, of course. "Everybody in the league knows what a pain in the ass he's been," said a team spokesman. Then, after leaving San Francisco for Miami, McKyer decided to burn every possible bridge he could think of, attacking 49er head coach George Seifert.

"He wasn't straight with me and I'm not ashamed to say that. I wouldn't play for him again. He could win 20 Super Bowls and it wouldn't change my mind."

The bad blood between McKyer and the 49ers—with McKyer being shipped off in the end—is typical of what happens to almost every pop-off sooner or later. Which makes you wonder how long Burt Grossman is going to last in San Diego. Or in football, for that matter.

Since he plays in San Diego, Grossman, a defensive tackle, is not as well known as some of the game's other leading pop-offs, but that's not because he isn't trying. For instance, he's apparently got a real thing against the Steelers, joking that if he'd been drafted by Pittsburgh he would have gotten himself frozen cryogenically for twenty years to avoid playing for them.

He also doesn't much like Steelers offensive tackle Tom Ricketts, a former teammate of Grossman's at Pitt. On hearing about Ricketts's wedding engagement, Grossman said,

"He just got engaged to a swimmer at Pitt. She's like 6'1", 200 pounds. So I said I wanted to put in a bid for their firstborn. I'd be set up for life. But I'd have to find somebody to take his SATs."

When informed that Ricketts didn't much care for his smart-alec remarks, Grossman replied,

"For real? Too bad he sucks and doesn't play. He'll never get to do anything about it. He didn't turn out to be what they wanted him to be, like every other first-round draft choice at Pittsburgh for the last 10 years."

After Grossman dumped on the Steelers one season, the next year he was asked for his follow-up assessment of the team. These were his words:

"A year's gone by but nothing's changed. Tom Ricketts is still on the bench, [linebacker] Jerry Olsavsky is still ugly, the Steelers still stink. And Tim Worley is an idiot."

The media loves the Burt Grossmans of this world because you can always count on them for a good quote. Here are a few more Grossman gems, directed at his San Diego teammates:

On All-Pro defensive end Lee Williams: "An amazing player. Old, but amazing. Led the AFC in sacks last year, but who knows it? If Lee had my personality, he'd be big time. He'll do newspaper stuff, but won't do TV interviews—and with that face I expect you know why."

On 300-pound assistant coach Ed White: "I'd say the guy's no heavier than the Valdez tanker."

On linebacker Leslie O'Neal: "He brings a Louis Vuitton briefcase with him to the locker room. Looks good, but there's nothing in it except maybe his own football cards."

Grossman is young, but he's starting to develop quite a reputation in the NFL as a pass rusher and a loudmouth. During his rookie year he was running after Philly quarterback Randall Cunningham when he suddenly threw up on himself in the Eagles backfield. Somehow it seems fitting.

6

It's a Hard-Knock Life: The Life and Times of a Professional Football Player

So you want your son to grow up to play in the National Football League? Naw, probably not. Chances are you'd just as soon he grew up to be a tennis player or a regular on the PGA Tour, where you can draw big paychecks and you don't have to live in fear of some 250-pound jacked-up-on-steroids special teams maniac ripping apart every tendon and ligament in your knee with his teeth.

Despite the glamour and the money, it's not easy being a pro football player. For one, there's the violence. And it's not just the fact that you risk a potentially career-ending injury every time you put on the pads, it's the *attitude* about injuries that's so scary.

> "If a man doesn't get hurt, he hasn't been playing hard enough."
> —Larry Wilson, former defensive back turned general manager

In other words: If you aren't limping, you aren't trying. Dan Hampton, who had so many operations in his career they used to keep a bed open for him at all times at Chicago General, believes this. He scoffs at the NFL's injury reports, which list players as probable, questionable and doubtful for the coming games. "They would be closer to the truth if the league made the categories Sissy, Pussy and Squirrelling Out," says Hampton.

In addition to the ever-present threat of being injured or permanently maimed, the NFL is not exactly the Civil Service in terms of job security.

> "A football player is like a prostitute. Your body is only worth something for so long. When it's no good anymore, nobody wants it."
> —Larry Grantham, ex-Jets linebacker

"When your tank is empty they get rid of you."
                    —Matt Snell, after being cut by the Jets

Most NFL players have the life expectancy of kamikaze pilots. As Jerry Glanville has said, the NFL stands for "Not For Long." You hear about the big stars a lot. They get their names in the papers and appear on the talk shows, ghostwriters pen their autobiographies, and the lucky ones stick around for years and years. But the majority of players aren't so fortunate. The competition is keen, and before you know it somebody has cleaned out your locker.

"Coaches see helmets and shoulder pads. The bodies are just stuffing. And they can fill in more stuffing whenever they need it."
                    —Pete Gent, author and former Cowboys receiver

That's another thing. You can be loyal to your coach, but that doesn't mean he's going to be loyal to you forever. He's got another agenda, and it may not include you.

"Football's most obvious contradiction is its failure to teach character, self-discipline and responsibility, which it claims to do. There is little freedom. The system molds you into something easy to manipulate. It is a sad thing to see a 40-year-old man being checked into bed at night."
                    —George Sauer, ex-Jets receiver

It is a rare coach indeed that treats one of his players as an equal. Mainly, they are treated like little boys.

"In pro football, as in high school and college, the only way the coaches can establish their authority is to treat their players as boys."
                    —Dave Meggyesy, ex-pro and football rebel

One of the tried-and-true motivational techniques of the coaching profession is to insult the players' lack of maturity, in order to get them to perform more to the coach's liking. Three examples among many:

"He's in horrible, horrible, horrible shape. He's going to have to grow up and grow up quickly. He doesn't even know how to hold his hands to catch a pass."
                    —Colts receiver coach Chip Myers,
                    on one of his players

"Aundray has got to grow up, on and off the field."
—Falcons coach Marion Campbell, after benching
No. 1 pick Aundray Bruce

"He says his hamstring is still bothering him and he can't run full speed. The next question is, why wasn't he in here for treatment? He said, 'I don't know.' Those kinds of things really disappoint us as coaches. He's a guy trying to get ready to play, claims he has an injury, never gets any treatment. He's got a lot of growing up to do."
—Sam Wyche, on wide receiver
Reggie Rembert as a rookie

Can you think of any other line of work except for the military where you would let your boss talk about you like that? But in football coaching, it's not only accepted, it's expected of you. Sam Wyche screamed, "You're a fucking loser!" at injured cornerback Lewis Billups because Billups was talking on the sideline during a practice, and Boomer Esiason said he didn't blame Wyche one bit. "The coaches aren't paid to be our friends," said Boomer. "They're paid to be our critics."

Coaches are also paid to be your baby-sitter, whether you need one or not.

"On the road we have a two-hour siesta time Saturday afternoons when we have to be in our rooms. This is ridiculous. We're grown men. Now do you know why I laugh? How can you take that seriously?"
—Steve Wright, on what it was like to play for the
Chicago Bears some years ago

When you bridle against the customary restrictions of pro football, as Steve Wright did, you are branded an ingrate or a flake or worse. Wright, who played for the Bears, the Redskins and other teams in his career, often argued with his coaches over what he saw as unnecessary rules and regulations. As he explained,

"I had a confrontation with Jim Ringo [assistant coach for the Bears] at the start. I told him not to give me any bull. If I do the job, play me, and if I don't do the job get rid of me, but don't bull me. Not playing is a bummer, but taking bull from a coach to make him feel good is worse."

Besides the sometimes petty rules a player must abide by, it's a fact of football life that he can be demoted or let go or traded without explanation or reason. Wright claimed that George Allen, the Washington coach, lied to him and then waffled about telling Wright that he'd been traded. Said Wright: "He lied to me and then was mealymouthed when he traded me—I had to say, 'Spit it out, George.' "

Other players have had similar experiences. Nose tackle Fred Smerlas was nudged off the Buffalo Bills roster even though, he said, he was outplaying the person who was being slotted to replace him. Smerlas looks back with bitterness:

"When I left there [Buffalo], a lot of people got crossed off my Christmas list. They tried to fit Jeff Wright into the shoe and it didn't fit. I outplayed him last year. It was creepy. I went to [head coach] Marv Levy and I said, 'What's the deal?' He said, 'He'll improve.' I told him, 'Who does your evaluating? He's not playing well.' If he was better than me I'd have gladly sat on the bench and tried to help him. That wasn't the case."

A coach is not obligated to explain anything. So Todd Christensen found out. A five-time All Pro, he was trying to come back from a knee injury and a gallbladder operation when he was released by Raiders coach Mike Shanahan. Said an angry Christensen after getting the pink slip:

"I didn't appreciate that after all these years. If indeed they were going to go in another direction, I should have been informed. Had I been allowed the opportunity to compete, and if [Shanahan] could look me in the eye across the table and say, 'This man is a better football player than you,' I could have lived with that. That didn't occur."

Christensen has since gone on to a lucrative broadcasting career, so we can put away the crying towel for him. In fact, the purpose of this discussion is not to drum up sympathy for these football players, many of whom are narrow, self-centered individuals who have led overly pampered, one-dimensional lives and who, because they happen to be able to run the 40 in 4.5, now possess fortunes that rival European royalty.

No, we are here not to bestow sympathy on those for whom sympathy does not apply. Our role is simply to shed light on aspects of the game that most fans may not have thought much about or have come to take for granted. In any case . . .

One aspect of the game that the pro football establishment doesn't like to talk about is racism.

"Prejudice is too common a commodity in professional football: routine, expected. Almost every team, for example, has a cell of white racists."

—Jack Olson, sportswriter

Jack Olson wrote those words for *Sports Illustrated* in 1968. Times have changed a great deal since then, inside pro football and out, but the nasty stain of racism still lingers. When Tony Dorsett broke into football he said he encountered "overt racism" from Dallas fans who wanted the black players to remain in "their place." Added Dorsett,

"In Dallas, in the late 1970s, white people didn't seem to have a problem calling you a nigger to your face."

A couple of years ago Jim Brown, the greatest running back ever, called the Pro Football Hall of Fame "racist" because of who it's keeping out. "How can John Mackey not be in it? How can Lynn Swann not be in it?" he said. "It's racist." Black quarterbacks are beginning to become more prevalent, but black general managers are nonexistent and black coaches remain a rarity. The NFL points proudly to Art Shell of the Raiders, but it's a crime that talented black assistants can hardly get in the door at colleges, let alone the pros.

"With Bill Walsh's recommendation, I couldn't get an interview at Kansas. With Bill Walsh's recommendation, Bruce Coslet [hired as coach of the New York Jets] and Mike Holmgren got interviewed by NFL teams. That shows you the difference."

—Sherman Lewis, longtime 49ers assistant coach

No matter what race you are, every NFL player faces certain indignities that he would likely not find in any other profession. There is the matter of the draft. Forget the All-American listings. A college player is ultimately judged by how high he is drafted by the pros, and if he is neglected completely and not picked at all, it's an insult that practically dooms any chance he has of making an NFL club. And if he's picked low, it hurts his salary prospects.

Thurman Thomas, the marvelous Bills running back, has never forgotten how he was picked in the second round of the 1988 draft, the 40th pick overall behind seven other running backs, including Gaston Green and Brad Muster. Thomas ridicules Green—"I've probably gained more yards in one game than Green has in his career"—but he becomes positively apoplectic about the Stanford man picked No. 23 by the Bears:

"Brad Muster shocked me the most. I look at guys like Brad Muster. Oh, I won't make any comment on that. . . . It could have been Neal Anderson and me in the Bears' backfield, instead of Neal Anderson and Brad Muster. I'm a hell of a lot better than Brad Muster."

Asked by a reporter what he had against Muster, Thomas said, "I got nothing against him. He's just Brad Muster," adding, "Are you trying to tell me Brad Muster went 25th and I went 40th and he's better than me?"

The great cornerback Lester Hayes, he of Raider fame, resented the fact he was not taken until the fifth round. Because Lester stammered people thought he was stupid. But, as he says,

"Some guys picked ahead of me couldn't even pronounce their names."

But Lester's biggest source of frustration with football did not involve his beginnings; rather it came toward the end of his career. Tied with Raider coach Willie Brown for a team record 39 career interceptions, Hayes felt that he was prevented from breaking the record and having it all to himself by members of the Raiders organization who wanted it to remain Willie's. Said Lester at the time:

"There are some individuals in Silver and Blackdom who would rather run through a gauntlet of pit bulls wearing pork chop underwear than see me break the record for interceptions by a Raider."

Plagued by injuries at the end and forced to retire, Lester never got sole possession of the record, and he resents Brown to this day:

"I was coached by a Hall of Famer who was an egomaniac. Can you imagine I had to deal with that every day, and I was the biggest egomaniac on the planet. It bored me. That's all we heard [from Brown], the way it was in 1968 when he was covering a Caucasian class of receivers wearing combat boots."

Complain as he might, Lester could've had it worse. A lot worse. He could've been a lineman. (Of course, he would've had to gain about 100 pounds.) Linemen don't ever get to intercept balls, unless it's a freak. Hell, they hardly even get to touch the ball. And Thurman Thomas may not have liked his draft position, but most linemen—even the good ones—have to wait until the later rounds, which reduces their bargaining power still more. And linemen can bitch all they want, but because they're linemen nobody is going to pay much attention to them.

So that's another thing to consider when you're assessing football as a potential career for Junior. There's always the possibility he could end up as a nose tackle or something like that.

"Nose tackle is a little like being a fire hydrant at the Westminster Dog Show. You've got all these pedigrees around you, and all you do is get pissed on."

—Jim Burt, nose tackle

The linemen are the grunts of football. The only time you hear about any of them is when the referee turns on his mike and says, "Offensive holding. Number 75." Then the camera shoots over to an embarrassed Number 75 who's saying, "Naw, no way. Never happened."

When Bubba Paris was a rookie he was known as "Highway 77"—his number is 77—because the quickest way to get to the quarterback was through Bubba. Now Bubba is known largely for his blubber, which is considerable.

"Paris has three weaknesses: breakfast, lunch and dinner."

—Ed Werder, sportswriter

For as long as he's been in the league the 49ers have been battling Bubba over his weight, which is in the vicinity of 325 pounds. Bill Walsh got so frustrated with Bubba that he replaced him on the offensive line with Steve Wallace, saying that "Wallace finishes his blocks, and not his plate."

Being a lineman is bad enough, being a fat lineman is to leave yourself open to mockery. "That guy was so fat it looked like someone sat in his lap and didn't leave," Jerry Glanville said about a 300-pounder he cut from his team, and Ron Meyer, coach of the Colts, was equally mocking about a pair of 350-pound-plus offensive tackles who reported to training camp. "I just hope they can get down in a stance," said Meyer.

The most famous fat person in the NFL is William "Refrigerator" Perry, who, as a teammate once said, is "just a biscuit away from 350." A defensive tackle by trade, the Fridge was a national phenomenon during the Bears' 1985 Super Bowl season because Chicago occasionally used him in the backfield to block and carry the ball, and because he couldn't stay away from those biscuits. After he made a couple of one-handed tackles in a game, a reporter joked, "Maybe his other hand was holding a sandwich."

His eating habits were a marvel to all, even his opponents. It was said that he ate five chickens a day, and prepared them himself:

"Last year he was skinning them. This year he's not even bothering to cook them."
> —Bill Fralic, Atlanta offensive guard who had to
> face Perry across the line

About the only person who seemed unamused by the Refrigerator and his booming national popularity was his coach, Mike Ditka, who said that Perry "believes that all there is to life is to make money, eat, get fat and die."

Like Walsh and Bubba Paris, Ditka challenged Refrigerator to lose weight. When William did not, and his play seemed to fall off, Ditka benched him in the season after the Super Bowl. Said Ditka, explaining the reason for his move:

"Folk heroes come and go. Just think about Davey Crockett. I haven't heard his name mentioned all week. You're only a hero when you're doing it."

Which brings us to another aspect of the football player's hard-knock life, perhaps the toughest of all to swallow. How quickly his fortunes can change. One day he's a hero, the next day he's history. But that's an entirely new subject, one that will be taken up in more detail in the next chapter.

7

From Chicken Salad to Chicken You-Know-What: How Fate Plays Havoc with the Fortunes of Football Teams

You roll the dice. Sometimes you roll a seven; sometimes it comes up snake eyes. That's true in life, and that's true for football players and the teams they play for. Nobody understands that better than the fine citizens of Buffalo, New York, a city that has long suffered under a collective inferiority complex.

Comparing his hometown of Miami with Buffalo, columnist Dave Barry wrote,

"Buffalo, a city whose major contribution to western civilization is chicken wings. . . . Buffalo, where the crime rate is indeed lower than Miami's because the getaway cars won't start."

They've heard all the cracks in Buffalo. With the possible exception of Cleveland, Buffalo is the city people most like to dump on. Gary Smith said that O. J. Simpson never belonged there because "he was a Maserati in a snowplow town." Then there was Bill Parcells's famous crack after the Giants had beaten Buffalo in Super Bowl XXV. Asked if he felt bad for Bills kicker Scott Norwood, who missed a last-second field goal that would've won it for the Bills, Parcells said,

"No, the only thing I feel bad about is that he has to live in Buffalo."

What made it worse for Buffalo is that for so many years their football team seemed to confirm all the cruel things outsiders said about their town. A joke:

"Knock, knock."
"Who's there?"
"Oh."
"Oh who?"
"Oh and 10."

They told that joke about the Bills, who liked last place so much they called it home. All those high draft choices they were picking up paid off, though, and they signed some outstanding talent. But all this talent couldn't get its act together, and people started calling them "the Fabulous Bicker Boys." After Bicker Boy Jim Kelly got sacked in a game and separated his shoulder on the play, he pointed the finger at a culprit on his offensive line:

"We have a good offensive line except for one person, and you know who that is."

That person was rookie lineman Howard Ballard, who had failed to protect his quarterback. But Kelly himself was considered to be part of the problem too. After losing five games in a row on the road, Thurman Thomas, the Bills' star running back, was asked what Buffalo's primary weakness was. "Quarterback," he said instantly.

The Bills were rolling snake eyes all over the place, but then something happened to turn it around for them. Fate? Luck? Maturity? Whatever it was, they went for a long, happy ride in 1990 that culminated with a stomping of the Raiders in the AFC Championship and ended with that near-miss in Super Bowl XXV.

Herschel Walker and the Minnesota Vikings should take heart from Buffalo's example. The worm *can* turn. Things can go from bad to worse, but they can also go from worse to great in the same space of time, and nobody but nobody will be able to explain exactly why either set of events occurred.

It's instructive to look back on the humongous 1989 deal that brought Walker to the Vikings. The Vikes gave up a ton of draft choices and some good players to get Herschel, but at first, conventional wisdom thought they got the better of the deal—

"If I was one of those Vikings and I had been traded, I'd be pissed. I don't know if I'd go. The Cowboys right now aren't going anywhere."

—Eric Dickerson, Colts running back

The Cowboys weren't going anywhere, and with Herschel running the ball the Vikes were going to the Super Bowl. Oh, how the fickle finger of fate can taunt us all! Some Viking players, however, weren't quite as sure that the thick-muscled former Donald Trump pinup boy was going to take them to the Promised Land as advertised.

"When we got [linebacker] Mike Merriweather, everyone said it was the missing link to get to the Super Bowl. Now, Herschel Walker is the missing link. How many missing links do we need?"

—Steve Jordan, tight end

Vikings GM Mike Lynn engineered the Walker trade and told the press that the only way to measure the success of the deal was whether or not his team made it to the Super Bowl. Oops. Even Walker's agent has conceded that the trade was one of the worst in NFL history.

Blame lies everywhere, but it has fallen mainly on the shoulders of the failed savior.

"I don't blame Mike Lynn for making the trade. He probably thought he was getting a legitimate NFL running back, not Mr. Full-Bodied Shoulder Pads, who is afraid to hit a hole with his nose facing the goal line."

—Letter-writer, *Minneapolis Tribune*

Top-selling T-shirts in the Minneapolis-St. Paul area have said, "The H-Bomb has landed in Minnesota," and, somewhat less wittily but more succinct, "Herschel Sucks." A joke circulating among Viking fans went like this: "What's the difference between a Butterfinger and Herschel Walker?" Answer: "A Butterfinger only costs 50 cents."

Much has been made of the fact that Walker, a track sprinter and a fine all-around athlete, is working out to make the U.S. Olympic team as a bobsledder.

"Is it really a surprise that Herschel Walker would excel in a sport where the idea is to go downhill?"

—Bob Sansevere, columnist

"Some guys go hunting on their days off. They go drinking, too. . . . Herschel went off to go bobsledding. The perception is this: He doesn't give a damn. He makes more than everybody on the team, and we gave up everything to get him. Guys want to see him

talk about doing what's right for the team. We want a Super Bowl so bad we bleed for it. What does Herschel want?"
—Viking player, as quoted in *Sports Illustrated*

Patrick Reuschel, a Minneapolis columnist, joked that the reason Herschel likes bobsledding so much is that "the sled has handles on it." Anyone who has seen a bobsledder go down a track at speeds of 100 mph or more might think it strange criticism, but O. J. Simpson once accused Herschel of lacking courage. Herschel, who has mostly retreated under the volleying directed his way, responded to this one:

"O. J. has never liked me. How do you measure toughness? Do you have to have your teeth knocked out?"

Well, that might go a long way toward impressing Mike Ditka, who likes his guy, Neal Anderson, far more than the more highly paid Walker:

"I'll take him any time, any day, anywhere against No. 34 in a Vikings jersey. When people pay a guy a million to leave, a million to come, a million to hang around and a million to practice, a car and a home . . . he [Anderson] is worth every bit of it."

Dan Dierdorf, the *Monday Night Football* announcer, said that Walker "has been more of a detriment than anything else." No kidding. The deal soured the entire Minnesota franchise—coaches, players, management and fans.

"This has certainly been one of the worst trades in NFL history. Not only has it been a bad trade for the Vikings, but it's been a bad trade for Herschel. He's lost his confidence."
—Peter Johnson, Walker's agent

"Their coaching staff is in chaos right now. Most of them didn't want Herschel in the first place. They would have been happy with Gary Anderson [at running back], who would have come a lot cheaper. But Mike Lynn wanted to improve with a big splash of a trade. The whole thing has backfired."
—NFL executive, as quoted in *The National*

Coach Jerry Burns was among the many Vikings who turned defensive in the face of all the Herschel-inspired criticism. After a reporter suggested that perhaps Walker wasn't working out as well as Minnesota fans had been led to believe, Burns snapped,

"Herschel Walker is everything I expected of him. Now, what expectations the guy on the street has, I can't answer for every stiff in the city."

Later offensive coordinator Bob Schnelker was criticized for the way Walker was being used, and Burns really got mad. You might even say bleeping mad:

"As long as I've got this [bleeping] job, Bob Schnelker will be the [bleeping] offensive coordinator. We can't be responsible for the [bleeping] blocking or the [bleeping] tackling or the [bleeping] guys jumping offsides. We have one dumb [bleeping] play by Alfred Anderson when his [bleeping] shoe is coming off. We're [bleeping] hollering to call time out, but we run the [bleeping] trap play and his [bleeping] shoe comes off. That ain't Bob Schnelker's fault."

But when things go as bad as they did for the Vikings, somebody's number has to be called, and it was Bob Schnelker's. He was fired after the 1990 season along with defensive coordinator Floyd Peters. Still, they might have been happy to go. The whole Vikings season was about as pleasant as a case of the clap.

"Finding a smiling face in the Minnesota Vikings' locker room was about as difficult as finding someone willing to invest in Joan Crawford Day Care Centers."
—Terry Boers, columnist, after a game in 1990

The unhappy Vikings bear a lot of similarities to the Denver Broncos. They're both proud football franchises that have repeatedly teetered on the edge of greatness only to the fall to the ground in a disgusting heap. Both the Vikings and Broncos have played in four Super Bowls and been squashed in four Super Bowls.

The latest Bronco disaster came at Super Bowl XXIV when they met the San Francisco 49ers. Some Bronco fans, remembering their team's previous three Super Bowl appearances, were hoping that their boys might somehow falter in the championship game and not make it all the way to New Orleans. But no, it wasn't to be.

"This time, the Denver Broncos said, it would be different. And they were right. This time, it was even worse."
—Bill Dwyre, sportswriter

It was clear almost from the opening kickoff that the fates—and the 49ers—were not going to be kind to these Broncos. Again.

"From the outset, the Broncos were not exactly a profile in courage. On the first play, quarterback John Elway threw too low. On the second, he threw too high. On the third, he ran for his life. Less than a minute into Super Bowl XXIV, it already was time for a Heimlich maneuver."

—Bernie Miklasz, sportswriter

Elway is a terrific quarterback except when he plays in the Super Bowl. The joke in Herb Caen's column after the game was that the California Department of Transportation was naming several overpasses and underpasses in his honor. *USA Today* said that Elway "couldn't hit the Great Wall of China." Sportswriter Monte Poole chimed in that Elway was "awful at the start and improved to dreadful."

But Elway was not alone in his awfulness. Everybody on the Broncos deserves equal credit.

"Never have so many players from one team played so badly in front of so many people. All this team needed was Wrong Way Corrigan."

—Bill Dwyre, sportswriter

"The Broncos didn't do anything that stopped the 49ers' offense except watch the game clock count down to 0:00."

—Ron Thomas, sportswriter

"The only thing Denver won was the coin flip."

—Randy Cross, ex-49er center

"You have to wonder if the Denver Broncos could have won the Bud Bowl."

—Randy Galloway, sportswriter

The score at halftime was 28–3. The game was over, but unfortunately they still had to play another thirty minutes.

"You kind of had the feeling the Broncos were whipped when they came running out on the field after halftime and two of them were knocked down by a trombone player."

—Jay Leno, comedian

Leno also joked that there were nasty rumors floating around the NFL that the Broncos had tested positive for Sominex. And David Letterman came up with these Top 10 cheers for the Broncos in the locker room at halftime:

10. Hold 'em under a hundred!
9. More magazines!
8. All we need is 25 field goals!
7. Oh, for the sweet release of death!
6. Drug tests! Drug tests!
5. Dig-ni-tee! Dig-ni-tee! Leave us our Dig-ni-tee!
4. Hey, that big San Francisco guy was shoving!
3. Start the bus! Start the bus!
2. Two, four, six, eight . . . Aw, screw it!
1. Wait till the Pro Bowl!

The final tally was 55–10, the worst beating in Super Bowl history. It was a nightmare that surpassed the fears of even the most pessimistic Broncos fans.

"The monkey climbed a little higher on Sunday. He got up around the shoulder blades, dug in his toenails and slipped a hairy chokehold around the Denver Broncos' collective neck. This team had wanted badly to shake the ignominy of losing the only three Super Bowls in which they'd played. They wanted to avoid, at any cost, the indistinction of joining the Minnesota Vikings as the only team in NFL history to drop four of them. But now the Vikings may not want to have anything to do with these Broncos."

—Eric Noland, sportswriter

The Broncos had done more than just lose a game, they had become a national joke. After singer Bonnie Raitt won her fourth Grammy at the nationally televised awards ceremony for the recording industry, emcee Gary Shandling cracked, "Here's an update on the scores: Bonnie Raitt four, the Denver Broncos nothing."

The unfortunate plight of author Salman Rushdie, driven into hiding by religious fanatics for a book he wrote, became another excuse for Denver Bronco humor.

"Salman Rushdie says he's had so much free time while in hiding that he's become addicted to watching American football. Next year maybe he can be at the Super Bowl and the Broncos will be in hiding."

—Bill Tammeus, sportswriter

And Tom Fitzgerald noted after the game that while Rushdie may be in hiding, he now had some company—the Denver Broncos. Ron Rapoport added that the Broncos had become "the

Typhoid Mary of sports" and expressed the wish, shared by virtually all, that in the future they stay away from any more Super Bowls. Said Rapoport:

"Everybody in the league will be rooting against the Broncos now for fear they might louse up another Super Bowl sometime. Compared to the Broncos, the Cubs are a success story."

Super Bowl XXIV was most definitely a dark, dark moment for the Broncos, but there may be another way of looking at it. Only the Broncos and the Vikings have ever lost four Super Bowls. Maybe that's not so bad after all, as Denver linebacker Karl Mecklenburg says:

"I grew up in Minneapolis. I followed the Vikings. They were a great team. Being compared to the Vikings is no slap in the face to me. It's much better than being compared to the Lions or somebody like that who never got there."

In other words, it's better to have gone to the Super Bowl and gotten your face kicked in than not to have gone at all. Some teams, don't forget, never get to the Big Show or even close. They don't ever flirt with greatness, they just wallow in the basement collecting No. 1 picks but not knowing what to do with them.

The Tampa Bay Buccaneers—aka the Tranquilized Bay Buccaneers, the Monstrosities by the Bay, the Tampa Bay Yucs—have not been horrible for all the years of their existence, but pretty close to it.

"I can't wait until the World League of American Football comes to Orlando. Then we'll have our own NFL developmental team—just as Tampa does."
                                  —Brian Schmitz, Orlando sportswriter

It doesn't seem to matter who coaches the Bucs; they play poorly. Until he was fired in 1990 their coach was Ray Perkins, who had previously developed losing teams at the New York Giants and the University of Alabama and thus was the perfect choice as head man for Tampa.

Not known for his sunny disposition anyway, Perkins had plenty to be gloomy about in 1990. And you have to sympathize with him as he suffered through yet another losing season—for him and for the Bucs.

After a loss to Dallas—

"At least we didn't get anybody killed."

After a loss to Green Bay—

"As a team, we didn't play well. In fact, we are a very poor team. We didn't play good enough to beat the No. 1-ranked high school in the state of Florida or Wisconsin."

After a loss to the Bears—

"I think offensively, we stunk. That's the whole bunch. Not just one person. We might just scrap our entire passing game and just start over from scratch."

After a loss to the Chargers—

"I can't get out there and play physical, but I can whip somebody's ass. . . . You know I might have to do that."

After a loss to the Vikings, when asked if he saw anything about the game he liked—

"No, but I missed the halftime show. That might have been good."

As the losses mounted, fans chanted "Throw Ray in the Bay" and wore bags over their heads. Ticket-holders organized a boycott, staying away from a game until the second quarter. Billboards in Tampa bill it as "America's Next Great City," but one newspaper wag said there wasn't a chance of that happening—not with Perkins in town. At one point all the pressure seemed to get to him, and he lashed out in a wild harangue against . . . the American way.

The American way?

"I make the decisions, and I can live by them. And I don't give a damn what anybody thinks. That's just the way I am. I've always been that way. Sometimes I don't do things the American way, but sometimes the American way stinks. I'm not part of the American way. I don't know why I am the way I am. I'm serious. Sometimes I wonder if it's worth being honest and doing what I think is right. The American way is to lie. The American way is to say things that people want to hear. Part of the American way is politics and I think politics is part of the reason this country is in the shape it's in."

After he was fired late in the season, a more focused Perkins directed his attack against the fans of Tampa Bay, saying,

"I would like to say to those people who exerted an awful lot of energy to try to get my head cut off, which was successful. . . . I challenge those people to exert that energy in supporting these Buccaneers. I felt like we had a home field advantage in one game the four years I've been here."

It remains to be seen how much support Tampa Bay fans will give to their team in the future. Probably will depend a lot on whether the Bucs can rise above the ashes of their past. As former Tampa Bay coach John McKay said after the Bucs lost every game in 1976, "We'll be back. But maybe not in this century."

But—make no mistake—they will be back. It's in the nature of the game, and it doesn't have anything to do with parity. We're talking something larger here, folks. Karma. What goes around comes around.

At one time Kansas City was so bad that after Mike Ditka had his heart attack, the joke was that he was going to be named coach of the Chiefs. See, his doctor ordered him to get as far away from professional football as possible.

Now the Chiefs are pretty good and seem to be getting better. After they get better, they'll get worse again. Count on it.

One year the Lions were so bad, said an opposing coach, that "playing them was like having the week off." When Jerry Glanville was an assistant there he swears the offense was so weak that "our longest run of the year was a huddle break." Now the Lions have the run 'n' shoot.

There was a football TV show in Phoenix called "1st and 10." People joked that the Cardinals' offensive line was called for holding so many times it should be renamed "1st and 20." The Cardinals could get better. So could the Indianapolis Dolts—uh, Colts. So could the Falcons. So could the Jets.

Why, even the New England Patriots could improve! It's not impossible. Stranger things have happened. And what could have been stranger than the season they had in, oh, let's say 1990, when they went 1–15 on the field and commited collective hari-kari off it? As one Massachusetts father wrote to his son, a Marine corporal stationed in the Persian Gulf prior to the Iraq war:

"I know it's rough over there. But look at it this way—at least you don't have to see the Patriots games over there."

8

Blood Feuds of Football: The Toe-Stomping, Kidney-Punching, Eye-Gouging Rivalries of College and Professional Football

If the Hatfields and McCoys had played a sport, it would have been football. They would have eaten it up. Because in football if you don't like the guys you're lined up against, you can not only beat them in the game, you can bash their brains out while you're doing it.

Rivalries exist in other sports, but except perhaps for the nationalistic savagery of world soccer, nothing quite matches football. In no other sport are the rivalries as strong, as long-lasting, as intense as in football. This is particularly true with the colleges. Oklahoma-Texas, USC-UCLA, Army-Navy, Texas-Oklahoma, Harvard-Yale, Notre Dame against everybody else, Miami versus their parole officers—these annual dustups are the delight of every season.

Down South, one of the best rivalries is Auburn-Alabama. In recent years Auburn has been getting the best of it, and rubbing it in every chance it gets. A joke: How many Alabama fans does it take to change a light bulb? Answer: Three. One to change the bulb and two to talk about how good the old bulb was.

Another joke: What do the Pope and Gene Stallings have in common? Answer: Both are ex-Cardinals who don't know a damn thing about football. Stallings, the Alabama coach, formerly was with the Phoenix Cardinals, and if you didn't know that you obviously haven't been following Alabama-Auburn. One more:

Why should Auburn play Alabama the first game of the season instead of the last? Answer: So they'd have all season to look for a new coach.

Fanatical followers of the Crimson Tide—there is no other kind of follower—do not appreciate such humor, but then Auburn partisans don't much appreciate the way they've been treated by Alabama all these years.

"Alabama fans don't want you to walk on the same side of the street as them. They want you in slavery. They want you in bondage."

—Pat Dye, Auburn coach

Being the coach of Auburn, Dye is not well-liked in Birmingham, the home of UA. When he was briefly hospitalized one season for a possible ulcer, the *Birmingham Post-Herald*'s headline read: "Dye still not dead."

Another long-standing and hard-fought rivalry is Michigan-Ohio State. Ohio State was coached for many years by the raging bull of college football, Woody Hayes. Hayes hated to lose, and he especially hated to lose to the men of Ann Arbor, but even more than these two things he may have hated the media. He held reporters in contempt and often confronted them physically.

"That ought to take care of you, you son of a bitch," Hayes said to a newspaper photographer during a 1973 Rose Bowl game, shoving the camera back into the man's face. The photographer pressed battery charges against Hayes that were later dropped when he apologized. Four years after this incident Hayes punched a TV cameraman in the face after the Buckeyes made a turnover against Michigan.

Woody's undoing came in the 1978 Gator Bowl and it involved not a member of the media, but Clemson linebacker Charlie Bauman, who intercepted a Buckeye pass in the last two minutes of the game with Ohio State losing 17–15. Woody lost control, pouncing on Bauman and throwing a punch in the melee that followed. He was fired the next day.

"People keep saying Woody Hayes is a great football coach who overstayed his time. This implies there was a time when slugging a member of the opposing team was proper coaching deportment. Let's face it, throwing a punch at Charlie Bauman of Clemson was only the last degrading incident in a pattern of behavior that had long distinguished the Ohio State coach."

—Red Smith, columnist

Hayes's counterpart across the sidelines at Michigan was Bo Schembechler, who has since retired from college football and moved into the front office of the baseball Detroit Tigers. The man Schembechler replaced as president of the Tigers was Jim Campbell, who played baseball for Ohio State when Bo was pitching for Miami of Ohio. The two have different memories, however, of what happened when they faced each other in a game.

"I can't tell you much about the game," Schembechler told an interviewer, "but I know damn well he didn't get a hit." Asked for his recollection, Campbell said, "I remember that fat little left-hander. He's so full of it. I hit three ropes off him."

Schembechler incurred the wrath of baseball fans when he was accused—unjustifiably, some said—of engineering the forced retirement of popular Tigers broadcaster Ernie Harwell after the 1991 season. One of those angered by the move was sportswriter Bill Madden, who described Bo as . . .

". . . A bullheaded old football coach kicking dirt all over a national treasure. We shouldn't really be all that surprised by Schembechler. In all his years as Michigan football coach perhaps no one other than his mentor, Woody Hayes, ever consistently showed less class on the American sporting scene."

Schembechler, said columnist Allan Malamud, is "finding the American League to be a lot like the Rose Bowl." That's a good line because, as Wolverine fans are painfully aware, Schembechler couldn't win beans whenever he and his boys journeyed west to Pasadena. But that's been the case with almost every Big-10 team over the last decade. The traditional rivalry with the Pac-10 has turned into a mismatch; witness Washington's romp over Iowa in the 1991 Rose Bowl offering.

"All season long, the Hawkeyes have worn the initials ANF on their helmets—America Needs Farmers. They should change it to INF—Iowa Needs Footballers. . . . It was another embarrassing showing by the Not-So-Big-Anymore Ten Conference. Penn State's membership in a couple of seasons will make it the Big

Eleven. But in Pasadena it remains the Big Disappointment Conference."

—Woody Woodburn, columnist

A frequent representative of the Pac-10 in the Rose Bowl is USC, or the "University of Spoiled Children," as it is also called. USC's greatest rivalries are with Notre Dame and UCLA across the city. The stereotype about UCLA is that it is populated by beautiful blonde coeds, while the stereotype about USC is that the football team is composed of knuckleheads.

"I love to watch the USC football players stand in line, because it looks like evolution."

—Byron Allen, comedian

"I understand the TV show 'That's Incredible!' has been filming on the USC campus. They shot 12 football players attending class at the same time."

—George Raveling, Washington State basketball coach who later came to coach at USC

But why pick on the Trojans (except that they make such a wonderful target)? Lots of schools have pretty dubious records when it comes to the educational performance of their alleged student-athletes. After running back Glyn Milburn transferred from Oklahoma to Stanford, Bob Sarlatte joked,

"When he was at Oklahoma, he was branded as a witch because he could read and write."

Oklahoma's chief rivals are Nebraska, Texas, and Oklahoma State. In past years, though, OU's biggest enemy has been itself. Wracked by drug scandals and various outrages committed by its players, Barry Switzer's program had gone berserk. Finally the NCAA couldn't ignore it any longer and put it in detention for a while.

Since leaving the school Switzer has been harshly criticized by two of his former players, both of whom wrote books about their experiences at OU. One of the author/critics was college big-shot, failed-pro Brian Bosworth. In Bosworth's book he skewers his old coach, saying things like—

"Barry Switzer is an insecure person . . . more insecure than almost anybody I know. . . . When he looked at me, he saw somebody he always wanted to be. The bigger I got, the more jealous he got. . . . The King [Switzer] loved to party. . . . The King is divorced and not because his wife didn't like his cooking."

Switzer once said that Bosworth was "a great player. I just didn't like The Boz, the media egomaniac." Referring to this comment, The Boz wrote, "The funny thing about that statement is that anybody that knows the King knows that the man is on the All-Time All-Ego Five."

The King was also attacked by a former Sooners quarterback, Charles Thompson, who, funny thing, was in prison when *his* book came out. In response, Switzer said that he had "never seen such filth and profanity" as in Thompson's book, describing its author thusly,

"Charles has no credibility at all. He is a sociopath, a criminal and an incorrigible liar. He is the scum of the earth."

Now, obviously such ravings have little to do with the grand old rivalries of college football, except to say: This is a game played with passion. For all their numerous (and in certain cases, indictable) flaws, Switzer, Bosworth, Charles Thompson and for that matter Woody Hayes all brought enormous passion to what they did, and that passion helped charge the games they played with meaning. Institutions do not cause rivalries to form and grow; individuals do.

In the pro game, there are lots of different kinds of rivalries—not just team against team (or school against school) as you mainly find in college. There are player rivalries, city rivalries, geographical rivalries, coaching rivalries, rivalries among owners, rivalries among members of the same team or between a coach and his players—the whole gamut.

Another type of rivalry is between the old and the new—when prima donna ex-stars criticize the prima donna current stars who have replaced them or somehow seem to be threatening their vaunted reputations. Jim Brown is a good one for that. To hear Brown tell it, there's never been another running back like Jim Brown and there never will be. Ask him about Bo Jackson and he'll tell ya,

"Don't ask me to compare myself to a half-a-season guy, who didn't have to play in the snow or with blood in his nose or every third-and-1. Bo Jackson is a very fortunate person . . . to have a coach who allows him to be a designated hitter and to have Marcus Allen, who's very accommodating."

Jim Brown was the greatest ever. If you don't believe that, just ask Jim Brown.

John Riggins was another case of that. After retiring he felt compelled to put the knock on the man who succeeded him at fullback, George Rogers:

"We'd run plays where there were arms and legs flying around in the holes, and you'd have to run. George doesn't want to run through that stuff."

To which Mr. Rogers responded:

"Riggins should keep his mouth shut. He's probably saying those things to get attention."

Coaches can be intensely jealous too. They're both retired now, but you can bet John McKay and John Ralston didn't exchange Valentine cards when they were active. McKay coached for USC when Ralston was at Stanford, and later they both moved up into the pros, McKay to Tampa Bay and Ralston to Denver. After McKay's Bucs crushed Ralston's Broncos in a 1976 game, McKay assessed his coaching opponent:

"He's a prick. He always was a prick. I hope he gets fired."

Yet another form of rivalry is the geographical rivalry, e.g., Cincinnati-Cleveland. A popular T-shirt sold in Cincinnati shows a Browns helmet and a Bengals helmet. Under the Bengals helmet, it says "This is your brain," while under the Browns helmet it reads, "This is your brain on drugs."

Browns fans are known as rowdies who often throw snowballs at opposing players from the stands. After a Cincinnati fan threw a snowball onto the field at a home game, Bengals coach Sam Wyche took a microphone on the sidelines and told the entire stadium,

"Will the first person who sees anyone throw anything onto the field, will you point him out so we can get him outta here? You don't live in Cleveland, you live in Cincinnati!"

The rowdy Browns fans also figured prominently in Cleveland's long rivalry with Denver. In a 1989 game, members of the Dawg Pound pelted the Bronco players with all manner of junk from the stands, including snowballs stuffed with batteries. This infuriated Broncos owner Pat Bowlen, who raged that—

"In my mind, Cleveland has the three worsts in the league. They've got the worst dressing rooms and they've always had the worst dressing rooms, and they've never been improved. They've got the worst field and they've got the worst crowd control and security."

Adding insult to injury, a referee ordered the teams to switch ends of the field to get the Broncos away from the barking dawgs in one end zone. This gave the wind to the Browns in the final period, enabling Matt Bahr to kick a game-winning 48-yard field goal for Cleveland. Bowlen went on—

"That situation over there [Cleveland] is a real bush situation. You look at the English soccer situation and some of the problems they have in England with the soccer crowds. We're not too far from that situation in Cleveland. . . . I don't know how they play baseball on that field, let alone football. I mean, we're over there in the first part of October and it ought to look like a golf course, and it looks like a cow pasture."

Browns owner Art Modell didn't forget this, and when he went to Mile High Stadium he complained that the owner's visiting box was so atrocious he had to spend $5,000 to fix it up. Bowlen replied that Modell's "biggest complaint is all the reporters can look in the window and see what he's doing. He has just as good a view as I do in mine."

Chicago and Green Bay have had a good rivalry, geographical and otherwise. They're both old-line NFL football franchises who play in the frigid North and whose traditions emphasize tough, hard-hitting football. But their rivalry flared in the mid-eighties when the Bears accused the Packers of dirty play under coach Forrest Gregg.

"Ever since Bart Starr left Green Bay, the Packers have been a bunch of thugs. The character of the ballclub is tremendously lacking. Overall, for that kind of attitude to permeate, something is lacking. They had high character when Bart was there. I don't see that anymore."

—Mike Ditka, Bears coach

Bears quarterback Jim McMahon echoed his coach's remarks after he was roughed up by Charles Martin on a pass play:

"I don't have much respect for Coach Gregg, and I don't have much respect for their players. I think they used to have a real good organization. It just seems to me it's gone downhill the last three or four years. I think Forrest Gregg has got to be a part of that."

Dan Hampton joined in too—"I wouldn't give you two cents for the whole Green Bay team"—but that was apparently as much as the Packers could take. After the Hampton blast appeared in the papers, a sack of manure was waiting beside his locker the next time the Bears came to town. A note was attached to it: "Here's what you guys are full of," it said.

Team rivalries such as Green Bay-Chicago or Cleveland-Denver tend to be more fluid in the pros than the colleges because they depend more on the quality of the teams involved. If the Broncos and Browns continue to stink up the joint like they did in 1990, nobody's going to care when they play each other. The Bears and Packers have more of a history together, but it's the same with them too. Unlike the colleges, where tradition counts for a lot, rivalries in the pros are based more on results.

Because they've both been so good in recent years, the 49ers and Giants have had one of the liveliest rivalries in the NFL. One of the best-ever *Monday Night Football* games involved the 49ers and Giants in a 1990 matchup, and anybody who saw it can't forget the way it ended: with Ronnie Lott and Phil Simms head-butting each other like a couple of stags in heat fighting over a doe.

One report had Lott calling Simms "a choker" during the game. And Simms, who once accused the 49ers of "laying down like dogs" in a losing effort to the Rams that cost the Giants a chance of getting into the 1988 playoffs, was pissed as hell about it in the locker room after:

"You play in this bleeping league 12 years, and you have to put up with this B.S."

Simms and Lott said it was all a misunderstanding, but later that season the two teams met again in the NFL Championship. While Simms and Lott kept their noses clean, in the week before the game 49ers tight end Jamie Williams explained how much he disliked the Giants because they had cut him as a rookie.

"It's going to be a personal vendetta for me, between me and the Giants. I feel that every play I do good, whether it's on special teams or a backside block or a five-yard catch, it's going to be a slap in the face to the guy who drafted me. Just them being the Giants is incentive enough for me."

When told about these comments, Bill Parcells, the man who drafted Williams, said dismissively, "He has been cut three or four times since. He plays about five minutes a game for the 49ers."

Williams, who's better known for his dreadlocks hairstyle than anything he's done on a football field, also said he didn't get along with Bill Belichick, the Giants' defensive coordinator who's now the top dog in Cleveland. Said Williams about young Bill:

"He's a guy I wouldn't mind meeting in an alley because of comments that were made. I never liked his style. I hope he doesn't venture out on the field when I'm there. He used to say things that if we were out in the street, he wouldn't say those things. [Those are] the kinds of things you hurt people for."

Jim Burt was a stud nose tackle for the Giants during their 1986–87 Super Bowl season, almost sawing Joe Montana in half with a brutal but legal hit during their 49–3 playoff rout over the 49ers that year. But a couple of years later the Giants cut Burt, and he was picked up by the 49ers.

Being cut or traded for the first time is like being jilted by a girl for the first time. You do not soon forget. Jamie Williams did not. Nor did Burt. On his first game back in New York as a 49er, he told reporters,

"I'll be looking for the fat guy with the headphones."

The fat guy was Parcells (who later went on a diet with some other NFL coaches and, according to the ads, lost 33 pounds with the Ultra Slim-Fast plan). Nothing came of Burt's threat, but in the championship game in 1991 he crashed into Jeff Hostetler's left leg and knocked him temporarily out of the game.

"We felt it was a cheap shot. That's the way Burt plays. He goes for the knees."

—Lawrence Taylor, Giants linebacker

Taylor was livid at what he saw as a "cheap shot." Enraged, he yelled at Burt from the sidelines: "If that's the way you want to play, somebody else is going to lose a quarterback." Parcells was yelling too, calling Burt "an asshole," and Giants nose tackle Erik Howard said it "motivated the crap out of us" in their tight, last-second win.

On the 49ers' next possession, they lost their quarterback just as Taylor had threatened. Leonard Marshall hit Montana with a clean, hard tackle, bruising Joe's sternum and breaking a bone in his hand. On the sidelines Taylor congratulated Marshall, shouting "How'd you like that, Burt?" across the field. In the locker room afterward Taylor described Marshall's hit as "justice."

Burt denied the cheap-shot charge, and films showing him being blocked into Hostetler by a Giants lineman appeared to back up his claim. Burt added that he was disappointed by some of the things the Giants had said because he was a former teammate of theirs and he didn't think they'd say those kinds of things about him.

But, as Burt is well aware, he was wearing the other team's uniform. Football is very tribal in that way. You paint your face and put on your colors and you square off against a tribe from another part of the country with different colors. And sometimes it gets a little ugly.

And when you talk about ugly, sooner or later you have to talk about the infamous "Bounty Bowl" involving the tribes of Dallas and Philadelphia. The source of the animus between the two teams goes back to the 1987 strike, when Dallas used some of its regular players to whip Philadelphia's replacement team. Eagles coach Buddy Ryan never forgave Dallas for this, and the next time they played he pulled a dirty trick on America's Team. In the closing seconds, with a Philly win already assured, Randall Cunningham dropped to one knee as if to down the ball, then sprang up suddenly and lofted a long touchdown pass to a sprinting receiver. Eat dirt, Cowboy scabs.

The feud got nastier still when Cowboys kicker Luis Zendejas, formerly with the Eagles, got knocked silly on a kickoff during the second half of the Philadelphia-Dallas Thanksgiving Day game. Luis, claiming that Ryan had told his players to get him, was not pleased:

"You know how Buddy is. If I could have stood up and decked him, I would have. The next time I can stand on my two legs and can get close enough to him, I will deck him."

After the Zendejas mugging, Dallas coach Jimmy Johnson charged that Ryan had put "bounties" on the heads of Troy Aikman and Zendejas. Knock one of them out of the game and you'll get a bonus—$200 for the placekicker, $500 for the quarterback. Ryan laughed off the charges: "I didn't know Dallas had anybody good enough to put a bounty on," he said.

The controversy spread, and while some people sympathized with Zendejas, many did not. It's a rough game, Luis. Even for kickers.

"If kickers are wearing pads and a helmet, then they should expect to get hit. If they don't they should take off the pads and run around in a pink uniform."

—Sam Huff, Hall of Fame linebacker

Bounty Bowl II occurred in Philadelphia a couple of weeks later and, although the Eagles won again, nobody on the Cowboys got beat up. Still, there were plenty of hard feelings. Dallas punter Mike Saxon was the target of snowballs from fans in the stands, and he claimed that Eagles tackle Ron Heller spit on him. Saxon said that he hoped Cowboy fans would retaliate the next time they played: "Maybe they can throw something at them in Dallas— something like cow dung."

And Luis Zendejas remained furious at his former coach and said so:

"I have two Christmas wishes this year. The first is to have 15 seconds alone in a dark alley with Buddy Ryan, so he would have to explain to me why he did it. The second is to have 15 seconds in the alley so I can beat the crap out of him."

The acrimony of the Bounty Bowl spilled over into the next season when the two teams met. Although nobody threw any cow dung, the two coaches did lob a couple of mud pies at each other. Said Ryan dismissively:

"They had a bad Thanksgiving Day game. Their coach, whatever his name is, instead of just taking the heat of a bad game, he made it into a Bounty Bowl."

And Jimmy Johnson replied:

"Maybe Buddy is getting senile, I don't know. He enjoys needling people and getting under your skin when he has the upper hand. You didn't see a lot of quotes earlier in the season when he was losing."

One footnote to the Bounty Bowl mess. A year after it occurred Dolphins utilityman Jim Jensen claimed that Ryan had put out a contract on him too. Jensen said that in Miami's game against Philly three Eagles had chased after him although he was well away from the play.

But in this case, Buddy was clearly innocent. Apparently Jensen had played in an off-season basketball game with some Eagle players and roughed up Philadelphia's backup quarterback, Don McPherson. The Eagles didn't like it and tried to retaliate on the football field.

Explained Ron Howard, the Eagles public relations director:

"This has absolutely nothing to do with Buddy Ryan. Our players just feel that Jim Jensen is a jerk."

9

Czar Pete vs. The Dictator: Rozelle, Davis and the Barnstorming Raiders

One of the nastiest and most hard-fought struggles in NFL history occurred not on a football field, but in a courtroom. It pitted Al Davis, owner of the Raiders, against Pete Rozelle, then commissioner of the NFL. On its face the trial was about whether or not the Raiders could leave Oakland and move to Los Angeles, but the real issue was power. The power of Rozelle and the league against that of Davis, who represented (in his mind) the right of an individual owner to run his franchise as he saw fit.

First, let's introduce the chief player in this test of wills, Al "Just Win, Baby" Davis. The Raiders are Al's baby, and they always will be (until he croaks or something). Coaches and players come and go, but Davis stays. He started as a coach of the Raiders back in the old AFL days, worked his way up to the executive suite and finally purchased controlling ownership in the club. The Davis philosophy is well known. As he has said, "This is a dictatorship, and I'm the dictator."

Not as well known is Davis's professed admiration for another famous dictator:

"He was a great admirer of Hitler and the Nazis. He and I would have these conversations and he'd call them 'a great organization' that 'drove their point home.' "
—Wayne Valley, former Raiders limited partner with Davis

Or, as Davis himself, who is Jewish, once told *Inside Sports:*

"I didn't hate Hitler. He captivated me. I knew he had to be stopped. He tried to take on the world."

So there's Al Davis for you. As Hunter Thompson has written,

"Any society that will put [Hell's Angels chieftain Sonny] Barger in jail and make Al Davis a respectable millionaire at the same time is not a society to be trifled with."

Larry Merchant has described Davis as a "gutter fighter." It was thought that Davis would do anything to win a football game, including installing hidden microphones in the opposing team's locker room to listen in on their game strategy. There is a story about a head coach who, deep in thought as his team was about to go out to play the Raiders in Oakland, suddenly erupted and started yelling at a light fixture in the locker room. "Fuck you!" he shouted. "Fuck you, Al Davis! I know you're there! Fuck you!"

Even among the non-paranoid, Davis was about as popular as a tick bite. A sportswriter had this to say about how he was viewed around the league:

"It is not at all certain where Al Davis would finish in a popularity contest among sharks, the mumps, income tax, and himself."

A former employee of Al's, back when the team was still in Oakland, talked about him to a magazine:

"He wants to be thought of as an athlete, but he isn't particularly well-coordinated. And he may have the skinniest pair of wheels in America, which is why he never takes off his pants where anyone can see. Then there's the Al Davis handshake. It's done with the fingers held apart and rigid so his little hand will seem bigger. He still wears those suits with the big padded shoulders. The players call him 'El Bago.' "

Reports have said that Davis has mellowed over the years, but he still keeps an iron grip on his team. After being traded from the Raiders during the '90 season, Vann McElroy blasted him:

"Let me tell you, it's like being let out of prison. It looks like he [Davis] has the players he likes and he has his players he doesn't like. And if you're a player he likes, he'll take care of you. Unfortunately, I wasn't one of those guys, and I got used as a sort of whipping post."

And, despite the alleged mellowing, Davis still has plenty of enemies around the league. "I'd rather not make any comments on Al Davis, not for a family newspaper," said Giants owner Wellington Mara when asked about him.

Davis is seen as an outsider among NFL owners. Partly because as a young man he looked and dressed like a cast-off from *Rebel Without A Cause.* Partly because his Raider teams—largely made up of outsiders themselves—played hard-nosed football and won championships. And partly because of his dictatorial, smarmy, sloganizing ("Pride and Poise," "Commitment to Excellence") personality.

But a good part of the animosity toward Davis—at least among his fellow owners—stems from his decision to take on the NFL's Powers That Be and beat them. Lured by the riches to be had in the nation's second-biggest media market and frustrated with negotiations in Oakland, Davis packed up and moved the Silver and Black to Los Angeles in 1982. This was in defiance of the rest of the NFL and specifically Pete Rozelle, the most powerful man in football.

Rozelle—"pro football's supreme being," as Red Smith called him—was a former public relations man who is widely credited with turning the National Football League into the premiere sports organization in the country. As commissioner, he guided football into the television age, oversaw the merger of the rival American Football League into the NFL fold, watched as football replaced baseball as America's top spectator sport, and set the stage for the league's expansion overseas.

Yet, in some people's eyes, Rozelle never strayed too far from his roots. Once a flack, always a flack. Gene Upshaw, head of the Players Association, described him as "a PR guy cloned as a commissioner." An NFL owner added that Rozelle could "be cold as a whore's heart, all the while flashing that PR smile." He was essentially a cheerleader—an exceptionally powerful and persuasive cheerleader, but a cheerleader nonetheless. His job was to boost the league and protect its image from the kind of damage that Al Davis was doing, or trying to do.

"I've always considered Al like a charming rogue, but in my business judgment, he's gone to outlaw."

—Pete Rozelle

Rozelle made this statement even before the Raiders had gone south to Los Angeles, a move that the commissioner said was in violation of league rules and could bring chaos to the NFL. Davis replied that the rules were illegal and Rozelle's charges a fear tactic:

"It's stupid. It's ridiculous. It's the same lament and cry from Rozelle and the other owners in the NFL for the last ten or 15 years. . . . Every time one of our illegal rules is struck from our constitution, it's meant 'doom' for the league. It's the old fear package, something that's typical of Rozelle."

Another of the arguments used against the move to LA was that Davis "owed something" to the fans in Oakland. But Davis said instead that the Oakland Coliseum was betraying the fans by not making the improvements he asked for:

"To hell with the Coliseum and the Coliseum board. They've been sold out for years . . . I know what they want. They want more money, and the question is how to get it. They care nothing about the people. It's a greedy organization, and I never thought I'd say that. It's a helluva thing for me to say. Most of the limited partners are friends of mine."

Davis ("the gutter fighter") and Pete Rozelle were natural enemies. Rozelle was a smooth operator with a high-handed way of dealing with people—"milk toast all over his high hand" was the way Cowboys owner Clint Murchison described it. Davis bristled at this and lashed out at Rozelle over the years with a series of scorching accusations:

"He had a nickname for a while, Sneaky Pete. He was called that in the league and he knows that. And that's the way he operates."

"I never have respected him. I've seen him flirt with the truth too often."

"I really don't think I would have had any problems if I wanted to move my team to Phoenix. I strongly believe that he wanted the [Los Angeles] territory for himself. Pete lived there, his family lived there. He wants equity. He doesn't want to be an employee, to have his salary docked. He's gotten older and he's reached a stage where he wants to play tennis, be a big socialite."

But a man as powerful as Rozelle is sure to have allies, and in this case, many of his allies were the National Football League owners who opposed Davis's move. They saw it as an act of rebellion by an out-of-control owner who was deliberately breaking the rules and staining the game's image. Jack Kent Cooke of the Redskins has called Davis "the dumbest owner in football." Besides Wellington Mara, Art Modell would probably not like to go on the record with his opinions about Davis. But unquestionably, Davis's chief enemy during this time—besides Rozelle—was Gene Klein of the San Diego Chargers.

Klein purchased the Chargers from Barron Hilton and quickly picked up a reputation as a man with a lively, outspoken wit. In 1976, for instance, a group that included Hilton filed suit to remove Klein as president and CEO of the Chargers. Klein was not amused:

"I paid Barron Hilton many millions of good American dollars, and now he wants to come back and run the club. This is quite stunning to me. . . . Most people know Barron doesn't have an overabundance of brains. The smartest thing he ever did was pick his father."

Klein was just as outspoken on the subject of Al Davis. Klein talking about Davis sounds a lot like, well, Davis talking about Rozelle.

"He's an asshole, and he wants to run the whole league. Rozelle had no choice about dealing with him. If you don't put a guy like Davis in his place, pretty soon you got no league left."

And:

"Mr. Davis is a clever man. Mr. Davis can talk in half-sentences. He can say several things in one sentence. Personally, I think that is by design."

Asked once if he "disliked" Davis, Klein replied, "Dislike? Hell, I hate the son of a bitch."

In 1981, while Al Davis vs. the NFL was still being tried in the courts, Mel Durslag of the *Los Angeles Herald-Examiner* wrote that the Raiders (then still in Oakland) were getting bum officiating, implying that the league was trying to punish Davis for wanting to come to LA. This infuriated Klein, who denounced Durslag as a lackey for the Raider owner. Quoth Gene:

"The afternoon newspaper in LA is an Oakland Raider mouthpiece. One of its columnists writes huge lies and makes incredible accusations. . . . It wouldn't have been a call from somebody in Oakland who asked him to write this—that couldn't happen, could it? I ask you, gentlemen of the press, if that's fair, equitable, honest reporting or is the writer in somebody's pocket?"

Klein did not stop there, adding:

"You know where it came from . . . a group of people who are practicing the big lie, the same thing that Hitler's people practiced, and Mr. Goebbels. You keep telling the big lie over and over again and pretty soon, people start to believe it. Throw enough of it at a wall and hope some of it sticks. That's nonsense."

To which Melvin Durslag responded:

"Mr. Klein is a deliciously scurrilous individual who takes the position that if you are not on his side, you must be crooked. . . . The National Football League is not above reproach, nor is Mr. Klein. All are fully capable, if not inclined, to punch to the pelvic region, describing people as being in the enemy's pocket, merely because they reject the political conspiracy that is keeping football out of Los Angeles. . . . Klein should be ashamed of himself."

In his defense Durslag might have also cited the NFL owner who, in talking about Gene Klein, said, "He's an authority on everything. He doesn't know a fucking thing."

In the end, Klein and Rozelle and the other owners lost and Davis won. In 1985 the courts affirmed that he had the right to move his team any place he liked, and the case was over. Afterward the victor had some advice for the vanquished:

"Rozelle needs to go to work and get out of the courtroom, get out of Congress, get out of the racetracks, get out of the social circles, get out of his vendettas, and be the commissioner again for the league. . . . I think for five years this guy [Rozelle] has done nothing but carry on this vendetta. All this energy, instead of spending it on the player strikes, promoting the game, new ideas, new concepts, this guy carried his vendetta to the ultimate."

Davis's sweetest moment in his dispute with Rozelle had to come even before this, when the underdog Raiders won the 1984 Super Bowl, and Pete awarded the Lombardi Trophy to him. There was some question in the media whether Rozelle and Davis would shake hands during the trophy presentation. They did. Then, over national television, Davis stuck the needle in one more time:

"Thank you, Mr. Commissioner. This is a great credit to an organization after all the outrageous things the league has done to it."

Ironically, especially considering how much trouble it took to prove that he had the right to go to Los Angeles in the first place, Davis very seriously considered junking LA and going back to Oakland. Actually, there was a time when Davis seemed to be considering moving to any place that would give him lots and lots of money with no strings attached and perhaps even build him a new stadium with all those luxury boxes he so desperately craves.

The "Return to Oakland" debacle offers further clues about the Davis mind and how it operates. Clearly, one reason why Al began shopping around again for another place to play was that the Raiders—the LA branch—had gone soft. The ever-colorful Lester Hayes, on his last legs as a player but a holdover from the Oakland days, summed it up:

"It seems like the Silver and Black has forgotten our Oakland Raider roots. There is too much handshaking going on and not enough eyebrow dusting. . . . Without the intangible of mystique we are a normal team. It distresses me. It causes mental malfunction. It bothers me to watch the mentality of the new Los Angeles Raiders."

Despite winning a Super Bowl championship after moving south, the franchise had steadily crumbled. A guy from Denver—Denver!—was brought in to revive the team. Why, the Raiders of yore—Stabler, Davidson, Otto, Tatum, Atkinson, the Mad Stork—used to eat guys from Denver for breakfast. Nobody was sure why, but that vaunted Silver and Black tradition seemed to be dying in the Southland.

"Halfway through the interview NBC's 'NFL Live' had with Al Davis last Sunday, I noticed my television set leaking oil badly. Imagine the guy saying, 'The Raiders have built a great tradition in Los Angeles.' "

—Phil Jackman, columnist

"The Raiders have a tradition, but it sure isn't here [Los Angeles]. . . . Oakland is a real town. Union. Blue-collar. Saturday nights, people go to bed early. Sunday mornings, they're off to the game. Monday, they go to work. Here, people stay up all night—

any night. The game's a social outing. And if the team isn't winning, they leave."
—Zeph Lee, Raiders cornerback who grew up in the Bay Area watching the old Oakland Raiders

Although there was apparently some sentiment among the Raider players for keeping the team in LA:

"In L.A., we have Jack Nicholson sitting on the bench with us. Who do we get in Oakland—a politician? As for the pretty ladies down here, wow. Much nicer to play with than dope dealers."
—Anonymous Raider player, as quoted in the
San Francisco Chronicle

Along with his worries over the "competitiveness" of his team—competitiveness was one reason Davis gave for moving originally—he was growing increasingly angry with the Los Angeles Coliseum for not delivering on some of the juicy things they had promised him. What happened to Davis there is similar to what occurred with Davis in Oakland. Much unhappiness over alleged broken promises. This prompted Al's wandering eye to go looking for prospective suckers in suburban cities with big ideas, such as Sacramento and Irwindale. Neither of these long shots quite panned out, so Davis deigned to have his pinkie ring kissed again by Oakland, which had never recovered from the time Al had jilted her before and still desperately wanted him back.

Oakland, a city suffering from bad schools, a high murder rate and extreme poverty, put together a $660 million sweetheart deal that Davis would've been a fool not to accept. Davis is no fool. While East Bay fans waxed ecstatic about the prospects of their heroes returning to Oakland, there were few regrets in LA:

"Are we surprised? If we are, we must be waking from a coma. Check his track record: Lie down with Al Davis, wake up alone."
—Mark Heisler, *Los Angeles Times*

"Should the Raiders move [to Oakland] for the 1990s? How about for the rest of 1989? How about if we help them pack, maybe make a few sandwiches for them so they won't get hungry on the trip?"
—Mike Downey, *Los Angeles Times*

But it never happened. People in Oakland balked at paying such a high ransom to get Davis back, and the deal encountered widespread opposition and ridicule.

"Why do I get this recurring thought? Al Davis goes alone into a room, locks the door and holds his sides laughing?"
—A contributor to Herb Caen's column, *San Francisco Chronicle*

"What a negotiator—he's the only man in California to get a prenuptial signing bonus."
—Buddy Baron, radio deejay

Chagrined Oakland city officials then put together a more realistic offer—only Davis shied away from that because it had to go to a vote of the people and, as is well known, dictators are not keen on votes of the people. Meanwhile, the Los Angeles Coliseum came up with a new package that seems to have placated its restless tenant, at least for the time being. The Raiders are staying in Los Angeles, and all is hunky-dory.

Or is it?

For a lot of people, and not just Pete Rozelle, the sight of Al Davis peddling his team to the highest bidder has not been pretty to watch:

"With the exception of Colts owner Robert Irsay, who in 1984 literally spirited his team away in the dead of night from Baltimore to Indianapolis, there is no owner, in any sport, who has operated with a more unseemly disregard for his constituents than Davis has. . . . Where there was once vision, there is now the slick veneer of opportunism. Where there was once devotion to football, there is a hunger for skyboxes. What Davis represents now is at best a failure of commitment and at worst a commitment to cynicism. And as for that old Raider pride, on which was built those championship teams? Just forget it, baby."
—William Nack, writer

10

The Wicked and the Damned: Conniving Owners, Gutless Players and the Bitter 1987 Strike

Apart from Al Davis, the man with the worst reputation among NFL owners is Bob Irsay, the loose cannon in charge of the Colts. Hey, but don't take my word for it. Listen to the people—including his ex-wife Harriet, who described him as "a drunkard and a compulsive gambler" when she filed for divorce—who've had dealings with the turkey.

"A liar, a cheat, crude, with no manners, and he drinks too much."
— Bert Jones, former Colts quarterback, on Irsay

"If you catch him before noon, you'll get a pretty decent answer from him, but after that, forget it. . . . Loyalty means nothing to them. I learned a good, tough lesson. Never trust management. They're all a bunch of liars."
— Pro Bowl guard Ron Solt, after ending a long holdout and signing a five-year, $2.65 million deal with the Colts

"Irsay has never contributed anything to the league since he's been in it. We would be better off without him."
— NFL owner, as quoted in *Playboy*

"His brain is baked. He's a jerk who says the dumbest things. You have to talk to him early in the morning or he's unintelligible."
— NFL front office man, as quoted in *The League,* by David Harris

Baltimore fans will never forgive Irsay because, among other things, he moved the Colts out of town.

"The Colts owner is an insecure man who deeply desires to be courted, a man given to royal tantrums when he doesn't get his way, a man prone to titanic swings in behavior. . . . [He is] a loud, brutish, erratic man who cannot be taken at his word, an interfering, miserly incompetent manager, a man who thrives on turmoil no matter the cost."
—*The Baltimore Sun,* 1984, before Irsay moved the team to Indianapolis

Irsay does say some fairly erratic things. In the late seventies, when Irsay first started threatening to leave Baltimore, he accused the governor of Maryland, Harry Hughes, of stonewalling him.

"The governor doesn't want to talk. . . . I guess Maryland elected God, not a governor. Well, I've had it with Maryland and the governor can go to hell."

The most disgusting thing Irsay ever said in public came when ESPN analyst Fred Edelstein predicted that Colts coach Ron Meyer would be fired after the 1990 season. Asked for his reaction, Irsay said about Edelstein,

"He's nothing but a little Jewish boy and he doesn't know anything."

Irsay later apologized for this slur, although surprisingly Edelstein wasn't that exercised about it. He said it was "just another dumb thing that Robert Irsay has said. If it was coming from George Bush or someone like that, it might have a little more impact."

Edelstein may be onto something there. What's so amazing anyway about the fact that Irsay acts like a jerk? As former NFL tackle Art Donovan says,

"I personally think that given the way he acts, he got hit in the head with a hand grenade. But it's his team, right?"

Irsay is not, after all, the first football owner to insult a public official or, sad to say, display a vile streak of anti-Semitism. Try to guess who said this:

"I'll tell ya, this is the last goddamned Jew I'm going to vote for. And only because he's replacing another Jew. You get too many of these sons of bitches and you've got a problem."

The year was 1969, and the man who said it was president of one of the most widely admired sports franchises in America. The occasion for the comment was the balloting by league owners to approve the sale of the Philadelphia Eagles from Jerry Wolman to Leonard Tose.

Give up yet?

The speaker was none other than the NFL's holy of holies, Vince Lombardi of the Green Bay Packers.

So let's never imply that stupidity or venality is restricted to a few misguided individuals like Irsay or Al Davis. Such qualities are spread liberally around the executive suites of the NFL.

As a matter of fact a number of owners currently operating professional football clubs have got the seven deadly sins memorized and are working on inventing some new ones of their own. Heartless? Some owners see their players as expendable as cattle.

"As long as attendance and TV revenue keep the money pouring in, owners will say, 'Why make changes? If players get hurt, so what? We'll get somebody else to play.' "
—Jon Morris, ex-NFL player

Dictatorial? Oh yeah, that too.

"If we told them to play on blacktop, the players would, because it's our game."
—An NFL owner, as told to Ed Garvey, onetime negotiator for the Players Association

And cheap? Tell us about it:

"He throws around nickels like they were manhole covers."
—Mike Ditka, on longtime Bears owner George Halas

All right, old George is dead and gone, but his Scroogian spirit lives on with another football legend, Paul Brown of Cincinnati:

"He treated his players as if he had bought them at auction with a ring in their noses."
—Jim Murray, columnist

An overabundance of ego is another common failing of owners. The dapper and urbane Leonard Tose, the former owner of the Eagles and the man who gained that grudging vote from Vince Lombardi, suffered from this.

The young Paul Brown "treated his players as if he had bought them at auction with a ring in their noses."

"Leonard Tose bought a sagging franchise to make money out of it to finance his own ego trips. . . . A man like Leonard Tose does not belong in the National Football League."
—*The Philadelphia Bulletin*

And the players agreed:

"I'll never complain again. Those poor Eagles really know what it's like to work for a slapped ass."
                    —New York Giants player, commenting on the
                                        Tose-owned Eagles

Owners have been known to stretch the truth as well. Or so said Leonard Tose himself about one of the legends of football, Lamar Hunt, the owner of the Kansas City Chiefs who founded the American Football League. Said Tose:

"How can I take a man's word for anything when he has totally disregarded his promises in the past? I won't put any more stock in what Lamar Hunt says at our league meetings, based on his performance, than I would in the man on the street telling me his opinion."

Tose was also unhappy with other aspects of Hunt's character, a criticism which may or may not apply to all owners.

"Lamar Hunt was a big disappointment. He has no balls."
                                        —Leonard Tose

Despite the obvious and many failings of the men and women who own the teams, most football fans try to ignore them as much as possible—that is, until they screw up so badly you can't ignore them any longer. One radio station in the Tampa Bay area erected a billboard with a picture of a giant screw next to the words HUGH CULVERHOUSE. Culverhouse is the owner of the long-suffering Bucs. Another radio station there held a contest in which people walked their dogs across a blown-up photograph of Culverhouse on the floor. The dog that pissed on Hugh's face or thereabouts was the winner.

With Irsay and Davis, fans in Baltimore and Oakland were mad at them because they moved their teams away. In the case of Bill Bidwill, people in St. Louis were just glad to be rid of him and even afraid he might come back if they built a new stadium.

"My worst nightmare is that we'll get this new stadium built and Bidwill will want to move the team back to St. Louis. The thought keeps me awake at night."
                    —Vincent Schoemehl, mayor of St. Louis

And when Bidwill was shopping around for a new place to play after growing disenchanted with St. Louis, people in Baltimore were ecstatic he didn't choose *them*.

"And now, when I think about it, I rate the greatest moments in Baltimore history thusly: The battle at Fort McHenry in the War of 1812. The Orioles' sweep of the Los Angeles Dodgers in 1966. The revitalization of the Inner Harbor. Bill Bidwill's decision to move to Phoenix."

—Mike Littwin, *Baltimore Sun*

According to columnist Lowell Cohn, Bidwill doesn't have "the brain of the lemon when it comes to football." Speaking of football owners, this is not as rare one would think. There is, for instance, Georgia Frontiere, who not only doesn't know anything about football but gets sensitive when people point it out:

"The owner, Georgia Frontiere, best known as a human Bermuda Triangle for husbands, had all the football organizational and strategical savvy of Charo. While unafraid to break new ground—Georgia was the first NFL owner to kiss players on the sidelines—Frontiere felt she was unfairly attacked by a sexist media and she retreated behind a wall of silence. She remains there."

—Scott Ostler, columnist

Unlike Frontiere, who's widely regarded as a cheapskate, 49ers owner Eddie DeBartolo, Jr., is accused of ladling too much money on his players, such as when he signed the USFL's Jim Fahnhorst to a $1.5 million contract in 1984.

"San Francisco is doing more harm than the USFL in escalating salaries. I don't know how they can issue a contract like that to unproven players, then look their 7-year players in the eye."
—Vikings GM Mike Lynn

DeBartolo, irritated at the criticism, issued a reply to Lynn:

"Tell him to mind his own business and try to build a winner up there. We've won a couple of Super Bowls. They've been a bridesmaid all their life."

DeBartolo may be an anomaly among owners because he is reputed to be well regarded by his players. More typical is Ralph Wilson. After Buffalo crushed the Raiders to win the 1990–91 AFC Championship, the Bills players got together and sang a song in the locker room in honor of Wilson, who has owned the team since its formation:

"Hooray for Ralph,
Hooray at last,
Hooray for Ralph,
He's a horse's ass."

But the hard fact about owners is that no matter how much they come to resemble the back end of a barnyard animal, nobody can fire them. And as long as they're around sticking their noses into things, things may never get better for their teams. When reports were circulating that San Diego owner Alex Spanos was going to hire the highly regarded Bobby Beathard as the team's next general manager, a former Chargers player didn't think it'd make a bit of difference as long as the tightfisted Spanos was in the picture.

"With the present owner, it's difficult to say who has a chance to do their job and do it correctly. I don't think Bobby Beathard is going to take the job unless he can have total control over the team and unless he can make some moves without having to call Stockton [where Spanos lives] or track down Spanos in some part of the country to decide if he can spend $20 to buy a typewriter ribbon."

—Kellen Winslow

Over in Cleveland, Art Modell is said to be a meddler too, a man who needs to sign off on the smallest details, and this is cited as one reason for the team's startling collapse in 1990 after playing for the AFC title the year before. During a loss against Houston a fan in the stands held up a sign that said "Jump, Art" next to a picture of Modell standing on the ledge of a building. The sign was quickly confiscated by security officers, but the next week a plane flew above Cleveland Stadium trailing a banner that read, "You Can't Touch This, Art."

Curiously, though, as much as we dislike owners and the things they do, football fans will almost always side with them in any kind of money dispute with players. For if there's anything we can't stand more than a deceitful, power-mad, money-grubbing owner, it's a whining, selfish, money-grubbing, over-pampered player who makes too much money to begin with.

Owners and general managers know this, and they used this to good advantage in the 1987 strike, one of the most bitter episodes in player-management relations in NFL history. That was when owners hired replacement players—or scabs, if you prefer—to

A guy who once ate quarterbacks for lunch, Mark Gastineau was just "another aging bum" at the time of the strike.

"I have one thing to say about the union. It's like Christopher Columbus. He didn't know where he was going. He didn't know where he was when he got there. He lost two-thirds of his ships along the way, and he did it with someone else's money."

—Matt Bahr, Browns kicker

Almost from the beginning, the players' ship began leaking. Some big stars crossed the picket line, including Giants linebacker Lawrence Taylor, prompting his teammate Robbie Jones to say:

"Anyone who follows Lawrence Taylor will burn in hell."

And Taylor responded:

"I'd rather burn in hell than spend five minutes in heaven with Robbie Jones."

Another prominent New York football personality to cross the line was Mark Gastineau of the Jets. The former sack-dancing showboat was, as Mike Lupica wrote, "once the most flamboyant defensive lineman in the game but now just another aging bum." Still, his defection from the ranks received wide publicity, and Gastineau justified it on the basis that he owed a certain responsibility to Leon Hess, owner of the Jets.

Gastineau's estranged wife, Lisa, could not let this pass without comment:

"Well it's very honorable to say, 'I have to fulfill my obliga-
tions.' Or to say, 'I have responsibilities.' But if Mark feels that
way, it would definitely be a change of personality. . . . As for my
daughter, he's gone three months without picking up the phone
to call her and four months without seeing her."

Gastineau was called "Scabineau" during the strike, and
berated by his colleagues around the league.

"He's a jerk and his teammates know it."
—Neal Olkewicz, Redskins linebacker

"What he's doing figures. Gastineau has an IQ of about room
temperature."
—Dan Hampton, Bears lineman

Someone from the Jets added that Gastineau's IQ wasn't equal
to his jersey number, because his number—99—was too high. And
Dennis Harrah of the Rams echoed this widely held sentiment
when he was told later in the year that he had made the Pro Bowl
team.

"I feel very fortunate to be [well liked]. I'd rather feel this
way than how people think about Mark Gastineau. Any man
who shaves his chest—I wonder what else he shaves? I feel very
fortunate that [fellow players] don't think I'm a puke like Gastineau."

But it wasn't just pukes like Gastineau who crossed. Joe Montana, idol of millions, caved in too.

"When he [Montana] crossed the picket line it bothered me,
because you had John Elway, who said, 'Hey I wanted to go back
in,' but he stuck it out. You had Phil Simms. I'm sure he would
have liked to collect the check. But he didn't go in. The Giants
stuck together. The same with Ken O'Brien. They all lost money.
You had these sleazebuckets like Lawrence Taylor who went in.
That's really bothered me. I thought [Montana] was more of a
man."
—Bob Rasmussen, co-writer of
Montana's book *Audibles*

Watching some of the biggest stars cross the line, as well as
many lesser players, the labor negotiator who had won so many
victories for pro baseball players was disgusted.

Joe Montana had the guts to withstand a fierce pass rush, but not stay on strike.

"My God, what wimps these football players are. What babies. It's sickening. Where's their resolve? They miss one paycheck or two, and they're ready to cave in? Gutless wonders is all they are."
—Marvin Miller, former executive director of the Major League Baseball Players' Association

But the footballers did not have Miller on their side, and after just three games with replacement teams, the regular players were crossing the line in such droves that the NFL Players Association had to run up the white flag. The players did get some concessions from the owners, but not authentic free agency and nothing close to what they had wanted.

The strike affected every team adversely, including Dallas, whose general manager Tex Schramm—one striking player called him "a moral-less person"—was chief water boy for the owners. In Dallas, Cowboy fans cheered more for the replacement players than they did the regulars, and when Danny White, the regular quarterback, took over for replacement QB Kevin Sweeney, the chant was sounded in Texas Stadium:

"White's a weenie. We want Sweeney!"

A number of Dallas regulars crossed the line, but when the other starters came back, they were furious at the thought of the scabs who had played in their place.

"If some scab had been in my locker, I would have thrown his stuff in the middle of the floor. Hey, I'll try to get along with them. But I won't share a locker with them."
                                    —Jeff Rohrer, Cowboys linebacker

"If I open my mouth I'll explode. The best thing I can do is keep it shut. I don't have anything kind to say about those people."
                                    —Eugene Lockhart, Cowboys linebacker

All in all, it's hard to find anything kind to say about the strike and all the bad feelings it caused around the league, especially among fans. As Buddy Ryan said at the time,

"I don't know who screwed this thing up, but it makes you want to throw up."

11

Exposé! The Bare Facts Behind the Lisa Olson Affair

The biggest name to emerge from the otherwise lackluster 1990–91 professional football season was not Jim Kelly or Bo Jackson or Jeff Hofstetler, although they all had pretty good years. The biggest name belonged to Lisa Olson, who did not gain one yard from scrimmage or make a single quarterback sack. But she was the focal point of a nasty piece of locker room business that will continue to haunt the people involved—not to mention the league itself—for years to come.

It came to be known as "The Lisa Olson Incident," although that's a shameful term because it puts the onus on her. It should be known as "The Day the New England Patriots Self-De-structed," or some such label that steers attention away from the victim and puts it where it belongs: on the guilty heads of Zeke Mowatt and his accomplices, the hapless New England organization, shaver mogul Victor Kiam and anybody else who contributed to the fiasco.

"See, the so-called Lisa Olson Incident did not become the so-called Lisa Olson Incident merely because of the events that took place in the Patriots' locker room on that September Monday. The thing took on a life of its own because of the way the Patriots chose to handle it, because of the way the *Boston Globe* and the *Boston Herald* turned it into a newspaper war . . . and because of the way *Globe* scoopmaster/television celebrity Will McDonough chose to spoon-feed his sneak-preview version of the Heymann Report to the masses."

—Steve Buckley, columnist

Yes, but that's getting ahead of ourselves. What happened on September 17, 1990, would have gotten Mowatt and the rest of his cronies arrested if it had happened anywhere else but in a football locker room. It was the day after the Patriots had beaten the Colts—their only win of the season, as it turned out—and Olson, a reporter for the *Boston Herald,* was interviewing a New England defensive back. As she was talking she noticed Mowatt coming toward her, so she hunkered down a little, fixing her attention completely on her subject.

There were shouts of "Make her look, make her look. Is she looking?" as Mowatt made his advance. Mowatt was naked. Lots of other people in the Patriot locker room were watching. It was all a big joke to them. The scuttlebutt on Olson was that she was "a looker," supposedly a reporter but really just a skirt who wanted to cop peeks at the gonads of real, live professional football players. She was just getting what she deserved.

"This entire episode was distasteful, unnecessary and damaging to the league and others. It included a mix of misconduct, insensitivity, misstatements and other inappropriate actions or inactions, all of which could and should have been avoided."

—Paul Tagliabue, NFL commissioner

Tagliabue issued this statement after a lengthy investigation into the incident, an investigation that corroborated Olson's version of events and thoroughly disgraced Mowatt's. "Not credible." Those were the words the polite special counsel used to describe Mowatt's testimony. Not only did the Patriots tight end expose himself to Olson, he lied when questioned about it after the fact. Then he hired himself a mouthpiece who made a big deal out of Zeke's taking a lie detector test and passing it.

"This exonerates Zeke and shows just how poorly this entire episode was handled. Zeke Mowatt was tried and found guilty in the press without getting a chance to tell his side of the story. What happened here is a disgrace."

—Robert Fraley, Mowatt's attorney

Fittingly, the lie detector test was mocked for the smoke screen it was:

"As for Zeke Mowatt and the 5½ hour lie detector test he took, why does it take 5½ hours to ask one question? Was the polygraph operator the same guy who makes the decisions on NFL instant replay calls? The test reportedly cleared Mowatt of all charges, but was the polygraph a Remington?"

—Scott Ostler, columnist

"To bring you up to date on the polygraph tote board, Zeke Mowatt has taken a lie detector test, Lisa Olson has offered to take a lie detector test, and Victor Kiam is expected to announce in a full-page ad that he liked the lie detector test so much that he bought the company."

—Tony Kornheiser, columnist

Kiam, the owner of the Pats, also owns Remington Products, which makes Lady Remington shavers for women. At one stage in the controversy Lisa Olson said of Kiam, "He's a joke, obviously," and Kiam did nothing to contradict this evaluation, getting himself into deep doo-doo for various stupidities he committed in the aftermath of the incident. The week after Olson's charges were made public, Kiam ran into Olson in the Patriots' locker room and gave this opinion of her:

"What a classic bitch! No wonder none of the players like her."

Kiam later denied saying this—he said he used the term "aggressive" to describe Olson—but he was overheard by two male reporters who said otherwise. Other comments of Kiam's are just as damaging. At one point he tried to dismiss the controversy "as a flyspeck in the ocean compared to the wider issues of football," and explained his position to the *Boston Herald:*

"I can't disagree with the players' actions. Your paper's asking for trouble, sending a female reporter to cover the team. Why not stand in front of her [naked] if she's an intruder?"

Kiam tried to paper over these remarks too, and do you think it had anything to do with the threats by NOW and other women's groups to boycott Remington? No boycott ever took place, but that didn't stop the ridicule. Lowell Cohn of the *San Francisco Chronicle* described Kiam as "a classic moron." *USA Today's* Weir joked that because Kiam was "in the razor business he felt obligated to act like a skinhead."

After hiring a New York PR firm to keep him from inflicting any more wounds to himself, Kiam took out full-page ads in several newspapers, issuing an apology to Olson and saying there was "no excuse" for the players' behavior. Kiam has said that he was never fully informed about what actually happened that day, but all of his statements on this matter have to be taken with heaping bags of Leslie salt.

A few weeks into the Gulf War, while addressing an all-male event in Connecticut, Kiam made this joke: "What do the Iraqis have in common with Lisa Olson? They've both seen Patriot missiles up close." Ellen Goodman didn't see the humor, writing in her column,

"Gag that man with a jock strap. One thought ran through the minds of even this friendly crowd, 'I can't believe he said that!' . . . Kiam has always reminded me of one of those nerdy kids who can't get anyone to play with them unless they have the only ball. He bought the ball, the playing field, the whole team."

Another appalling aspect to the affair was the reaction, or lack thereof, from the Patriots players and team representatives in the locker room. If Kiam didn't get the full story right away as he claims, it wasn't because lots of people weren't on hand to witness it. Both players and team officials did nothing as Mowatt came up to Olson and said, "Here's what you want. Do you want to take a bite out of this?" They stood by as Michael Timpson and some others laughed and egged him on. They watched as a few of their teammates, naked themselves, walked by Olson to see if they could get her to look. Terrified, she kept her head down as running back Robert Perryman "adjusted" his genitals—the special counsel's word—and wiggled his hips at her. Finally, Olson managed to escape with Perryman's taunting words chasing her out the locker room door: "If the kitchen is too hot, get out."

Inevitably, the widely publicized incident revived the old "Should women reporters be allowed in the locker room?" debate, with many NFL players predictably saying no.

"It's an invasion of privacy. It's indecent. You might as well interview me while I'm sitting on the pot."

—Roy Foster, Miami Dolphins

"How would members of the press feel if we came to their houses with a video camera and asked them questions while they were getting ready for work and showering?"

—Trace Armstrong, Chicago Bears

At least one player, however, professed not to care one way or the other:

"I don't care. I treat every reporter the same, like crap."

—Mike Baab, Cleveland Browns

One Miami TV station, trying to get its own angle on the controversy, ventured into the Dolphins locker room and showed pictures of players in almost all of their glory (their private parts were blocked out). Tim McKyer was shown wearing nothing but a jock strap. Viewer reaction was not favorable. The debate even reached into Congress, when Wyoming Senator Alan Simpson asked on a radio talk show,

"In the name of civil rights or the public's right to know, does America ask old Ted Kennedy to hold a press conference in his birthday suit?"

Kennedy responded:

"To stop the notion of women reporters in the locker room from getting your goat, Al—stop acting like an old goat yourself."

As if the issue didn't have enough nuttiness attached to it already, Sam Wyche of the Cincinnati Bengals decided to get involved too. Or, as Ray Ratto refers to Wyche,

"Slingin' Sam Wyche, the spotlight-grabbing, show-me-a-parade-so-I-can-jump-in-front-of-it leader of the Cincinnati Bengals."

Making his own statement on the issue, Wyche barred a woman reporter from the Bengals locker room after an October 1 game against the Seahawks. Wyche said he received numerous letters and expressions of support from the public for his stand as well as donations of money to help him pay the fine he was assessed for breaking league rules. The media, perhaps remembering how Wyche had knocked a microphone out of a reporter's hand after a 1986 game, were not as apt to climb onto Coach Sam's bandwagon.

"The Pro Football Writers of America strongly objects to the closing of the locker room to the media. We remind Coach Sam Wyche that he does not live in Beijing, he lives in Cincinnati."
—Don Pierson, reporter and president of the PFWA

"Sam has a dirty mind. He's also a bully. Plus, he's a bad loser. Other than that, he's a prince of a fellow."
—George Vecsey (*The New York Times*), who has also described Wyche as a "poor lummox"

"Spotlight-grabbing, show-me-a-parade-so-I-can-jump-in-front-of-it"
Sam Wyche got in on the women-in-the-locker-room controversy, too.

It's important to point out that whether one thinks Sam Wyche is a jerk or a brave fighter for the rights of football players to walk around a locker room with their balls hanging out and no women around, has nothing to do with what happened to Lisa Olson. Wyche's gripe is over policy; what Zeke Mowatt did was the act of a bully.

"By now, we should realize that the issue of women in the locker room is a phony dodge. The issue is that men can humiliate women and worse and still believe they can get away with it. The NFL, by the way, did little to discourage that notion."

—Mike Littwin, *Baltimore Sun*

Yet another sideshow was the sorry performance of reporter-turned-TV personality Will McDonough, whose reporting on NBC indicated that Zeke Mowatt was but an innocent lad, unjustly accused, who was simply not the type of individual who would walk around flaunting his ding-dong like that. McDonough was heavily criticized for these reports, and he defended himself in turn in his column in the *Boston Globe*. His brethren in the media were unforgiving:

"The McDonough report took the offensive. In the *Globe* on Friday, he rambled on with his version of events, but for all his posturing and get-tough talk, it was just a smoke screen of rationalizations. It was the Checkers speech of sportswriting. In 1,800 words of sticking his chest out, the words 'I made a mistake' never appeared."

—Norman Chad, television columnist

"Does NBC's Will McDonough—on the radio in New York this week doing damage control—actually think anyone believes that he was really on Lisa Olson's side all along?"

—Mike Lupica

In the end, this is what happened: Paul Tagliabue, NFL commissioner, fined Sam Wyche $27,941, one game's check, for breaking league rules and barring a female reporter from the Bengals' locker room. For his actions in the Patriots' locker room Zeke Mowatt received a $12,500 fine from Tagliabue but no suspension. Robert Perryman and Michael Timpson got $5,000 fines apiece. The Patriots organization was also fined $50,000. The disparity in Tagliabue's administering of "justice" in the case—the Wyche fine opposed to Mowatt's—did not go unnoticed.

"It was kind of like Sam is being charged with murder when all he's committed is a misdemeanor. And they [the Patriots involved] are being charged with a misdemeanor when they committed a felony. I have to think that what happened in New England was a hell of a lot worse than what happened with us in Seattle."

—Boomer Esiason, Bengals quarterback

"Tagliabue might as well have meted out the punishment—if you want to call it that—with a wink, a nudge in the side and some sly comment about guys being guys."

—Mike Littwin

"Earth to Commissioner Tagliabue: Is that all there is? You commission a special counsel to spend two months investigating the incident and subsequent events, your noted Harvard Law Professor interviews 91 witnesses, issues a 60-page report which basically substantiates all the bad things everyone was accused of, and you hand out fines as though these guys were late for the team bus?"

—Scott Ostler

Nevertheless, Olson pronounced herself satisfied with the Heymann Report, if not the severity of the punishment, and wished that the whole disgusting episode would go away once and for all. She is not alone. L'Affaire du Zeke helped poison New England's season, bring down a good coach (Rod Rust), severely damage a number of careers, add still more tension and animosity to the relationship between the press and athletes, give a black eye to the sport, and worst of all, hurt a person who wasn't doing anybody any harm and was just trying to do her job, for chrissakes.

About the only good thing I can think of that came out of the incident was that it brought back an anecdote about Mark Gastineau, the loudmouth former Jets defensive end. Some people said they wished Olson had handled it the same way, but that's not fair—again, it puts the burden on the victim, not the perpetrators where it properly belongs. Anyway, it seems that Jenny Kellner was in the same boat as Olson—a woman reporter, in a locker room, interviewing football players in various stages of undress. Only Kellner worked for the *New York Post* and her beat was the Jets.

While in the locker room one afternoon, Gastineau spotted the woman taking notes and approached her. He was buck naked. Nor was he shy. He stood right in front of Kellner and asked, "What do you think?"

Kellner looked up and said with a mixture of disdain and boredom,

"It looks like a penis, only smaller."

12

Commie Subversives, Failed Novelists, TV Clowns and Other Media Matters

Football and TV were made for each other, kind of like pretzels and cold beer. One of the immutable pleasures of the game is being able to sit home in the comfort of your living room and throw things at the people announcing the games on TV, people such as John Madden:

"TV viewers deserve educated analyses of plays and players, not annoying babble from Madden, who all too frequently interrupts his co-announcer to say things like, 'I tell ya, he's a heckuva football player. I tell ya.' Madden destroys the finesse side of football by claiming players are good only if they are fat, bloody, blubbery guys who eat raw meat. His on-screen scrawling is confusing, pointless and draws even more attention to the fact that, I tell ya, he's a heckuva slob. I tell ya."
—Letter-writer to *Sports Illustrated*

Madden is one of the more popular TV guys; not as many people seem to pick on him. Brent Musburger isn't so lucky. When he was fired as host of *NFL Today,* it was the best thing to happen to football since the invention of helmets.

"I don't think this many people have been as happy about a guy losing a job since Richard Nixon resigned."
—Ray Frager, columnist

One of the all-time worst TV sports promotions were those ridiculous Bud Bowl commercials, which made everyone associated with them look like idiots.

"I don't care about Bud Bowl, and I don't want to know about Bud Bowl, and the only time I watch one of those lame commercials with Chris Berman, it's because I can't find the remote for my television fast enough. I like Berman, but I'm going to have to level with him: Putting on the funny helmet has not been a sparkling career move."

—Mike Lupica, columnist

Television personalities are much like your in-laws; there are some of them you just can't stand to be in the same room with.

"Why does anybody pay attention to ESPN NFL analyst Fred Edelstein? Can anybody remember the last time this guy was right about anything?"

—Glenn Dickey, columnist

"When he told me I'd been a bad husband in my first marriage, it took everything I had to keep from jumping out of my seat at him."

—Terry Bradshaw, himself a TV personality, on being interviewed by ESPN's Roy Firestone

"Are college football commentators Pat Haden and Bob Griese clones, or what? Short ex-quarterbacks, high-pitched voices, smart, good guys, bland."

—Tom Gilmore, media columnist

Then there are the guys who stand on the sidelines during college games purportedly to give us inside dope on what's going on with the teams. These are the guys who really drive Tony Kornheiser up a wall:

"Half the time when they cut to these guys, we miss a touchdown. They're all camera hogs. They launch into a dissertation about a sprained ankle like they're Sir Richard Attenborough: 'I'm here, knee deep in mud by the Clemson bench, pondering what the limits of human endurance might be. This man, this swift, mercurial runner, has just been stung by one of fate's cruel darts . . .' and blah blah blah. How many plays will he miss, bozo? Is he out for the game?"

And let's not forget those sports talk shows, on radio and television:

"Just eliminating one discussion of the NFL draft on one sports talk show would keep 500,000 pounds of hot air from being released into the atmosphere and contributing to global warming."

—Peter Leo, *Pittsburgh Post-Gazette*

Every TV announcing team has a straight guy and an ex-jock. The ex-jock, or jockcaster, is there to lend credibility and an expert's eye to the goings-on on the field. He's been *there,* you see, so he knows. But isn't it curious how when you put these ex-jocks up in the booth with all their supposed expertise all they do is say the same innocuous, cliché-ridden things?

Lately, perhaps to get away from the Tweedledumbo-Tweedlediddly syndrome, TV has been pushing its announcers to give us hard-breaking, front page–type sports news—the inside poop, as it were. So what if so much of the stuff they come up with turns out to be false?

"Now for the latest stats in that scummy scrimmage among cable and network television's pro football inside-information specialists: Zero for the season. None of their great scoops has come true. Ah, but that's show biz. Or should we say show B.S.? . . . C'mon, guys, get real. If that's the kind of insider information you are going to report, then put David Leisure, aka Joe Isuzu, on the air with a proper label at the bottom of the screen—'He's lying.' "

—Frank Cooney, sportswriter

Bill Walsh, who apprenticed as coach of the 49ers before moving onto jockcasting, was hired by NBC not to break news, but to say lively and controversial things, which he has done. Some of Walsh's opinions have not been received kindly, such as when he said he thought the gimp-legged Dan Hampton should get out of football before they wheeled him out on a stretcher. Take it, Bill:

"He shouldn't be playing football ever again. He talks about his knees—they're so stiff he can't walk. The day before the game, they have to be drained. Every bit of cartilage is gone. He has arthritis. What will he be doing in 20 years? . . . He's going to be in a wheelchair unless something's done."

Walsh added that he hated to see Hampton get a sack, "because it means he'll think he can still play. It's the worst thing that can happen." Asked to comment on these remarks, Hampton, who did retire after the 1990 season, said,

"I can remember when Joe Montana came back after back surgery and a lot of doctors said if he gets another hit in the back, he'll be crippled for life. Walsh didn't tell him not to go out there. I think [Walsh is] a big hypocrite and a fool."

Hampton's coach, Mike Ditka, weighed in with his thoughts:

"Everyone is entitled to their own opinion. Sometimes I don't think before I talk. I don't know what was said. It's not my place or Dan's mother's place to tell Dan what to do. . . . You know Bill—he's got an awfully high opinion of what he is and what he does. It looks like the 49ers really missed him a lot, so what can you say?"

Walsh said much the same thing about Phoenix quarterback Neil Lomax as he did about Hampton, saying that he was washed up and should get out of the game:

"It's over for Neil. He will not be able to play the game again. He knows it's over. He hates to face it because he loves the game. . . . The sooner he releases it, releases his own emotions and steps away, the better for the Cardinals."

Lomax, who was suffering from a bad hip (the reason for Walsh's remarks), was hurt by what was said:

"I don't know where he got his information or how well he knows my condition. I don't know why people keep picking on me. I don't need that extra stuff. I don't need to think about my condition. I want to think about football. If you notice, there were no quotes from me. It was just his opinion."

It was also Walsh's considered opinion that the 49ers could go unbeaten during the 1990 season, which drew this reaction from Dan Reeves of the Broncos:

"They can and will be beat. There are a lot of things Bill says that I don't agree with. After watching his commentary the other day, it's amazing how much smarter he's gotten [since retiring]."

Amazing! But it happens to everybody who journeys up to the broadcast booth from the playing field. After serving as GM of the Redskins, Bobby Beathard signed on as "expert analyst" for NBC. Paid to say controversial things, he once accused Howie Long of the Raiders of going downhill as a player. Howie did not take kindly to this:

"We're just as responsible for Bobby Beathard being on TV as anyone. We kicked their butt just about every time we played them and those are the players he scouted and drafted. We traded them everyone but [equipment manager] Run Run Jones. And we were about to lock that deal up when he left Washington."

Jockcasters like Walsh and Beathard (now GM for the Chargers) are no different than the sportswriters on your local fishwrap or, for that matter, the guy sitting at the end of the bar with his face in the peanuts. Everybody has an opinion. So what if sometimes these opinions are harebrained? Who cares? That's the great thing about sports. Even the harebrained can participate on an equal basis. In fact it's nearly impossible to distinguish the harebrained from the not.

For the past two decades the most important TV football show—and, at times, the most harebrained—has been *Monday Night Football.* The current crop of *MNF* broadcasters includes Al Michaels and Dan Dierdorf, whom Buddy Ryan described thusly:

"One guy is an overweight lineman who doesn't know his head from second base, and the other guy is a soccer announcer, isn't he?"

Dierdorf is the talkative former lineman of the Cardinals who's a bit on the beefy side:

"Working definition of hell: the middle seat on an airplane, between Dan Dierdorf and Roseanne Barr."
—Mark Whicker, sportswriter

As *Monday Night*'s answer to John Madden, Dierdorf's job is to entertain and to give his opinions, not all of which are appreciated:

"That's disgusting. Who does he think he is? I've seen some of the horseshit teams he's played for."
—Jim Finks, New Orleans GM, after Dierdorf put a
bag over his head on television to show his disgust
for a *Monday Night* game

The other member of the *MNF* crew is marbles-in-his-mouth Frank Gifford, who has been on the show nearly as long as it's been on the air. Frank may be showing his years—or maybe he just talks that way naturally. In any case, CBS and NBC have play in place of the striking regulars. This caused an enormous schism among players and coaches, and turned off millions of fans.

As is well known, professional sports owners of any kind do not like unions or player associations. They resent the power that players have, and they resent having to pay such huge salaries to them.

"I don't know what the hell the players want anyway; they're making so much money now. Most of them are overpaid."

—Vince Lombardi

Lombardi said this in 1967 upon hearing the news that the players were forming a union. Since then management's attitude has changed very little. In 1970 John Mackey, then president of the NFL Players Association, called Rams owner Carroll Rosenbloom to tell him that a strike was possible. Astonished at this act of defiance, Rosenbloom told Mackey that the owners didn't need football—"But you do." An insulted Mackey in turn told Rosenbloom that, like most owners, "If you didn't have tickets to give away, you wouldn't have any friends."

Rosenbloom hung up on Mackey, but the hostility lingered. Players affiliated with the union were dismissed as Bolsheviks in shoulder pads, and teams tried to get rid of them. In 1974 the players went on strike and an irate Norm Van Brocklin, coach of the Falcons, told Ken Reaves, the team's player rep: "You and your picket sign are going to New Orleans!" That same year the Bears traded away three players, including team representative Mac Percival. Exulted George Halas:

"This is the greatest thing that's happened to the Bears in five years. We got rid of those malcontents. It's a great day, a great day!"

Normally the NFL owners can't agree on whether the sun comes up in the east or the west. But in 1987 they all united behind a fiendishly brilliant plan to put the squeeze on their regular players by hiring replacement squads of NFL rejects, semi-pros, ex-college athletes, as well as some ordinary guys whose dream had always been to play in the pros.

While the owners presented a united front, the players were split. Many did not want to go out on strike at all, and some resented the Players Association ostensibly working on their behalf.

reportedly talked about scrambling their signals on pro football telecasts to prevent pirating. ABC, however, is not considering such an action, and one columnist thinks he knows why:

"ABC, disdainful of costly new technology, in effect already scrambles its *Monday Night Football* signal by using Frank Gifford as broadcaster."

—Norman Chad, columnist

The Giffer was the straight man in the booth during *Monday Night Football*'s prime, the years when Dandy Don Meredith and Howard Cosell were on the show. The key word there is "show" because *MNF,* among other things, changed the football television business. No longer did they simply broadcast a football game; now it was . . . show biz! Lots of jokey, opinionated banter among the emcees, camera shots of girls in the stadium, slickly produced halftime highlights show, interviews with celebrities—the game of Nagurski and Grange and Amos Alonzo Stagg gone Hollywood.

MNF still has its moments, but in the beginning it really was something new and fresh. The banter between Dandy Don— "He's just telling us 'They're number one,' " he joked after a fan gave the finger to the camera on a telecast—and Howard Cosell was pretty entertaining schtick at times, though admittedly not everyone's cup of tea.

"If we wanted that kind of stuff, we'd put Jack Benny, Don Rickles and Bob Hope in the booth. But we're not going to sink to that. We're not running a comedy hour."

—Bill MacPhail, head of CBS Sports, on *MNF* with
Dandy Don and Howard

In today's *MNF* lineup Dan Dierdorf occupies the Dandy Don role, but there can be no substitute for Howard. He's off the show now, and there's no replacing him. Thank God, some would say.

"There have always been mixed emotions about Howard Cosell. Some people hate him like poison—and some people hate him just regular."

—Buddy Hackett, comedian

Cosell had a voice, as somebody once wrote, "that had all the resonance of a clogged Dristan bottle." He said lots of big words, often misusing them, and he was constantly reminding us in his clogged, Dristan bottle of a voice how important he was and how, really, a man of his breadth of intelligence and understanding ought to be senator or governor and not covering a childish little football match.

"He doesn't clarify or amplify, he CLARIFIES and AMPLIFIES. What comes at you is this: THIS IS ME, HOWARD CO-SELL, WHO JUST THIS AFTERNOON HAD LUNCH WITH CHOU EN LAI, TELLING YOU THAT THAT PASS WAS OVERTHROWN!!! Yes, we know, Howard, we just saw it."

—Larry Merchant

Howard prided himself in telling it like it is. Sometimes he did; sometimes he didn't. He described Lions head man Joe Schmidt as "a once great player, who as a coach, couldn't inspire a frog." He once referred to President Nixon as "Tricky Dick" on the air, and called the Redskins' black receiver Alvin Garrett "a little monkey." (Cosell was castigated for this remark.) In the first year of the program, not feeling well, Cosell tried to buck himself up with a couple of vodka drinks, then threw up on Dandy Don's cowboy boots. He left the telecast at halftime.

It may or may not have been this incident that led Jets coach Weeb Ewbank to say about Howard:

"That guy is libelous. On top of that, he can't drink."

Another time Cosell said that Warren Wells was flanked out wide for the Oakland Raiders, although at the time Wells was serving time in San Quentin for rape. Dandy Don later called this "the great escape." But Howard took himself very seriously, and he personally took much of the credit for the success of *Monday Night Football*. In his book he referred to Frank Gifford as "a male mannequin" and mentioned that Meredith "rarely prepared for a telecast."

After Meredith left the show in 1973 (he came back a few seasons later), ABC tried replacing him with Fred "The Hammer" Williamson, the cornerback turned action movie star. But after he commented, "Even an old cripple like you could have made more yardage through that hole, Howard," he was fired in the pre-season. A decade later O. J. Simpson was in the *MNF* announcing booth, and after a Cosell comment, the Juice gave voice to what millions of viewers had been thinking and saying for years:

"Howard, you've proved once again you have a tremendous grasp of the obvious—to use one of your lines."

One of Howard's most bitter antipathies—now there's a Cosell-type word for you—was the press. The feeling was mutual. Sportswriters frequently carved him up like so much Thanksgiving turkey, and he responded with flashing knives of his own. But in this regard, at least, Cosell had plenty of friends. Lots of football people—players, coaches, front office—carry animosity for those esteemed knights of the keyboard.

"I have nothing to say to a bunch of whores."
> —Giants linebacker Lawrence Taylor, dogged by a group of reporters asking about his marital problems

Reporter: "Are you in pain?"
Jim McMahon: "Only when I look at you."

"They've gone from a good newspaper to a junk newspaper. They've had me misquoted all year. And then they actually print deliberate lies. I should have a suit against them for blasphemy or something."
> —Mike Ditka on *USA Today,* after the paper said that the Bears coach had become "enraged" during his first post–heart attack game

"I check all the papers and find out what the consensus of opinion is and then try my best to go against that. It's the only fun I have."
> —Lindy Infante, Packers head coach

Bill Parcells, in a team meeting, once equated reporters with "Communist subversives." Bill Walsh told a group of corporate executives "how lucky you are not having to deal with sportswriters." Before a Super Bowl in New Orleans agent Leigh Steinberg announced he was hosting a party for the media on board a boat, which caused this crack from George Young, the Giants GM:

"When I heard he was taking all those writers out on a riverboat in New Orleans, I spent about an hour trying to see if I could rent a submarine."

Asked if he studied basketweaving in college, Joe Namath said, "Naw, journalism—it was easier." After having brain surgery, Norm Van Brocklin explained the purpose of the operation:

"It was a brain transplant. I got a sportswriter's brain so I could be sure I had one that hadn't been used."

Pursued by reporters in the team parking lot, Deion Sanders yelled out to a passing police car, "Can I press charges against these guys who never wore a jock and think they know all the answers?" (No, Deion, you cannot. Those are the rules.) Asked by a reporter if he was motivated to win the AFC West title, the Raiders' Bo Jackson snarled,

"Is this your first interview? Is this? How can you ask that question? Listen, if my mother was on the other side of the line, I'd want to run her over. I've never been to the playoffs. I want to see what it's like. Does that answer your question?"

Reporters do ask dumb questions. And they run in packs, like dogs raiding trash cans in the middle of the night. And depending on the prevailing winds, they do change their minds quite frequently.

"First I'm great, then I fumble, then I don't like to run inside. Half these guys have never put on a uniform."
—Eric Dickerson

After fumbling three times in a game, Dickerson left the locker room refusing to speak to the press. "Maybe his throat was sore from coughing up the football," commented one writer. And that may be what irks football people the most. No matter what, sportswriters always have the last word.

"If most sportswriters were any good at what they did, they would be novelists instead of sportswriters."
—George O'Leary, Georgia Tech defensive coach

Well, that's probably true. But what the heck. It's a living.

13

Issues and Answers: Are the Refs Dumb and Blind? Is the Run 'n' Shoot an Excuse to Hire Midgets? Does God Follow the NFL? These and Other Pressing Issues Explored

ISSUE NO. 1

Are football referees a bunch of blind, bubble-headed incompetents, or is this just the best we can expect from people who work part-time and on weekends?

This is a hotly debated question, especially after numerous blown calls in NFL games and that famous Colorado-Missouri boondoggle in which the referees granted Colorado a fifth down that enabled the Buffaloes to score a touchdown and win the game.

They're griping in the colleges—

"I thought the refereeing was miserable. We've been flagged for holding on first down five consecutive possessions inside the Nebraska 20 over two years. It's just too often. If you see us holding, call it at midfield but don't let me get all the way down the field and play this high school game."

—Iowa State Coach Jim Walden, after an away game at Nebraska

"You're going to have officiating like that, you might as well just let a damned old computer run the game. . . . I see a referee

using a spittoon for a hat, and I see a referee whose head's not going to be in the game the next day."
—Howard Schellenberger, Louisville coach,
knocking the refs after the Cardinals
lost in the John Hancock Bowl

And they're griping in the pros. When he was coaching for Cleveland, Bud Carson called the refereeing "a sad commentary." Others have been more forthright:

"Referee Ben Dreith and his crew were horrible, and the league office might want to consider issuing them mini-tricycles, big floppy rubber feet and plastic carnations that squirt water, because if they're going to act like [clowns], they might as well look like them."
—*Steeler Digest*

"Everyone is cognizant of the general deterioration of officiating. Things are just not uniform."
—Norman Braman, Eagles owner

"How come one crew has called 43 holding calls, and another has called three?"
—Dan Henning, Chargers coach

"It was so cold in Green Bay on Saturday that officials wore ski masks. With the kind of season they're having, it wouldn't have been a bad idea for them to wear them every week."
—Allan Malamud, sportswriter

During a *Monday Night Football* game, Dan Dierdorf observed, "Hey guys, that's another horrible call by the refs." And Al Michaels said, "They've had a lot of practice." Buddy Ryan described one ref's call as being so stupid "my wife could have made that." (Buddy's wife was not asked for her opinion of this comment.) Marv Levy in Buffalo said, "I hope it doesn't come to the point where I start mentioning specifically officials' names who don't do their jobs." Sam Wyche in Cincinnati asked the press after a game, "Let's see a show of hands. How many think the referees did a good job?" (No hands were raised.) When a reporter then asked Wyche what he thought of the refs, he said he had to hold his tongue, "but obviously you guys think they did a terrible job."

But this sort of thing isn't new, is it? "Given half the chance I'd punch one of them out," Mean Joe Greene said once about the officials. "And it'd give me a whole lot of satisfaction." Fred Arbanas, the ex-Chiefs tight end who had one eye, was asked by an official what he'd do if he ever lost his sight in his good eye. Said Arbanas: "I'd be an official just like you."

Football players and coaches have been baiting the refs since the game was invented. What is different, though, is that nowadays you've got television and the instant replay, which turns every bleary-brained, pot-bellied couch potato at home into an eagle-eyed observer willing to sink his talons into the hide of any referee at the first sign of an error. Which raises more interesting questions, namely:

ISSUE NO. 2

Is the instant-replay rule worth keeping around, and if it is, how do you light a fire under those stiffs up in the booth so they'll come to a decision before hell freezes over?

"Those guys don't know what they're doing. He was probably out getting a cup of coffee. I don't know what he was looking at."
—Vikings coach Jerry Burns, upset over a ruling by
a replay official

"We said we wanted to eliminate human error, but you just get more humans and more errors. We still have controversy. I don't think the officials on the field have to have eyes like they're from Krypton. I don't think we need a microscope. It's a human game."
—George Young, Giants GM,
criticizing the replay rule

"Stevie Wonder could have seen that I didn't have that ball."
—Dolphins receiver Mark Clayton, after a pass he
dropped was ruled a fumble by the replay officials

Despite the grumbling and the incessant second-guessing it fosters, the instant-replay rule will probably stick around. But this still doesn't answer the question of what to do with the guys in the booth who take so much time to make up their minds and still aren't sure about it.

"If I were on trial for a murder I had committed, I would want an all-replay official jury. Even if the prosecution had film of me pulling the trigger, I would get off. 'Inconclusive,' they would say. 'The hole in the head is obscured.' "
—John Eisenberg, columnist

ISSUE NO. 3

Is the run 'n' shoot here to stay, or is it just an excuse to give jobs to a bunch of midget wide receivers?

When the run 'n' shoot was just starting out, and most people thought Mouse Davis was some kind of Saturday morning cartoon character, a lot of powerful NFL thinkers dismissed it as a gimmick.

"I like Mouse, but the run 'n' shoot won't fly at this level."
—Marv Levy, Bills coach

"The run 'n' shoot is no big deal. NFL coaches would take about two weeks to figure it out, then it'd be like every other offense in the league. We'd stop the damn thing. Will it work in the NFL? Sure, it might. For a weekend."
—Buddy Ryan

Despite the skepticism, a few non-establishment football types thought that Mouse Davis's creation would work, and challenged the stick-in-the-mud NFL to give it a try.

"People are just too pansy to try it in the NFL. But I know it will work in this league. Mouse should be a head NFL coach."
—Jim Kelly, who quarterbacked the shoot in the
USFL before going to Buffalo

"The NFL is nothing but one guy copying another guy. That's why Mouse isn't an NFL head coach yet. A guy with original ideas scares the pants off the conservative NFL. Mouse knows how good his system is, so he sticks to his guns."
—Neil Lomax, a run 'n' shoot quarterback at
Portland State before joining the pros

It's still too early to tell whether this "half-baked, backyard fire drill," as Rick Reilly put it, will make it in the NFL. It's had some successes and some failures. In training camp in 1990 Chuck Knox in Seattle was calling his version of the run 'n' shoot "the spread." After the Bears shut the Seahawks out in the season opener, Chicago tackle Dan Hampton said a better name for it would be "The Chuck and Duck."

Whether or not the shoot, or some variation of it, survives over the long haul is anybody's guess. But it's already given a boost to the game. If nothing else it's added an element of excitement to the moribund (except Barry Sanders) Lions offense, and it represents a fresh idea and a new way of doing things, something the starchy NFL can use more of.

Take Sam Wyche's no-huddle offense. That, too, was written off at first by the football establishment, including Marv Levy, who's now one of its foremost proponents.

"Just because Vince Lombardi huddled, does the rest of the NFL have to huddle? If Lombardi jumped off a cliff, would the rest of the NFL follow? Whatever happened to originality?"

—Mike Bass, sportswriter

The answer to that is, NFL coaches and teams don't give a damn about originality. They just want to win.

"If a team wins the Super Bowl and someone asks them how they did it, and they answer that the players all wore two left shoes, the next year, every team in the league will wear two left shoes."

—Jerry Glanville, Falcons coach

ISSUE NO. 4

Is it in the nature of every NFL controversy to blow over after a year or two like it never happened in the first place?

Good question. The run 'n' shoot debate will probably be like that. Although the instant-replay rule is showing some staying power. But what about the anti-noise rule, which caused so much noise a few seasons ago?

Home teams were going to be penalized if their fans yelled too loudly, and this caused a big outcry.

"The integrity of the game is jeopardized because the people who are held accountable for the game—coaches, administrators and players—have no control over the fans. The fans now have a way to flaunt authority, and not be penalized."

—Ron Meyer, Colts coach

"Tell you what's going to kill that nonsensical anti-noise rule in the NFL. When the networks notice that the home team has lost all its timeouts and they can't slip in commercial after commercial during the usually protracted last two minutes of a half and at the end of a game, wham, it's gone."

—Phil Jackman, columnist

"I've asked the fans on my radio show, rather than make all the noise, just make some real nice signs. I think it's a dumb rule."

—Jerry Glanville

"Ticket holders and people pay $25 a ticket, and you're telling me they can't express their feelings? That doesn't seem fair. That shows you how much of a monopoly the NFL has."

—Dexter Manley, defensive lineman

The controversy was muted somewhat after the referees were given more leeway to decide when to penalize the home team for an overly rambunctious crowd. In Los Angeles, however, the anti-noise rule was never much of an issue with Rams fans.

"The only time they make angry noise is when Nordstrom runs out of suspenders."

—Mark Whicker, sportswriter

ISSUE NO. 5

Is the NFL a hypocritical organization, as some allege, or is it a repository of goodness and virtue, as no one alleges?

The hypocrisy question exploded onto the front pages of America—as the tabloids like to say—when the NFL decided to yank the 1993 Super Bowl out of Arizona after that state voted not to honor Martin Luther King's birthday as a holiday. Many in and out of the game applauded the league's move.

"Arizona doesn't deserve the Super Bowl. The state doesn't deserve it if they can't do the right thing. This will put us in a category as being a lowlife state."

—Eric Hill, Phoenix Cardinals linebacker

But others accused the league of hypocrisy and meddling in politics.

"The NFL sells tickets to Democrats, it sells tickets to Republicans. The NFL sells tickets to criminals, sociopaths, left-handers and people who snore. It sells tickets to teeth-pickers, pinkos, droolers, litterbugs, parking violators and folks who spit on the sidewalk. A guy doesn't have to be politically correct to buy a football ticket. Why must a state be that way (in the NFL's opinion) to host a game?"

—Paul Daugherty, columnist

Others thought the league did the right thing but was still hypocritical.

"As far as being hypocritical, I don't want to insult the NFL, but yeah, they are. But the NFL is a business, first and foremost. A business has to make business decisions, and the NFL made the right one."

—Castle Redmond, Cal Berkeley linebacker (whose team decided to play in the 1990 Copper Bowl in Arizona)

This issue was so big, even the Indians got into it.

"If the NFL were really motivated by ethnic concerns, why would they have a team called the Redskins? What if some other team came into the league and decided to call themselves the Blackskins and the Yellowskins? I and [other] American Indians . . . are forced to conclude that your concern about the lack of a Martin Luther King holiday is strictly business motivated and has nothing to do with race consciousness."

—David Moore, president, American Indian Bible College

Another issue that has called into question the NFL's ethical and moral standards is drugs. The league argues that it has developed a sane and humanitarian program to deal with the cokeheads in its lot. Some are not so sure.

"Athletes are breaking the law and hiding behind the NFL banner. They go to a 30-day rehabilitation program while the guy on the street gets thrown in jail."

—Sam Huff, former All-Pro linebacker

"Know what a lifetime sentence for drug offenses means in the NFL? It means one year if you're Dexter Manley. Three times and you're out for 12 months."

—Bob Verdi, columnist

Dexter did get off relatively easy, but shortening his suspension and allowing him to play shows mercy and not vindictiveness. On the question of steroids, however, the position of the NFL is unflinching. It is absolutely and unequivocally opposed to their use and has introduced testing programs to identify and ferret out any of the juiced-up rascals.

"I read in the newspaper yesterday that the National Football League suspended 13 players for testing positive to steroids. Then

I fell on the floor laughing. Only 13 steroid users in a sample of 2,200 players? Get serious. There are probably individual teams that have 13 steroid fiends right now. I bet some teams have even more."

—Lowell Cohn, columnist

"The league's attitude about dealing with the [drug] problem reminds me of how my father dealt with sex. Mean looks and lots of no talk about it."

—Harlan Svare, former NFL coach

All right, there may be tinctures of hypocrisy in this attitude, too. But come on, guys, what's the big deal about steroids anyway?

"You have to question the effectiveness of steroids now that Northwestern football players have been accused of using them."

—Allan Malamud, columnist

ISSUE NO. 6

Speaking of hypocrisy and holier-than-thou attitudes, where does Notre Dame get off anyway?

In 1990 the Fighting (and Money-Making) Irish signed an exclusive five-year $38 million deal with NBC to televise its games. This was a shocking deal to many people. The college game's biggest attraction had opted out of the televised package governing the College Football Association and was striking out, loot in hand, on its own.

"I wasn't surprised by this, I was shocked. Surprise, shock, greed and ultimate greed. That's the reaction I'm getting from people."

—Vince Dooley, Georgia athletic director

You can say that again, Vince. Judging from the reaction of most non-Notre Damers, you'd have thought the Irish were breaking up the Gold Dome and selling it for scrap.

"To me, Notre Dame has vacated its leadership role. This is greed."

—Frank Broyles, Arkansas athletic director

"They said they were doing it for their fans and alumni, but I don't think there was a real big problem seeing Notre Dame on TV. I call it greed."

—Rudy Davalos, Houston athletic director

"The bottom line is money, and it boils down to one word: greed. Notre Dame wants all the exposure and all the money."

—Oval Jaynes, Colorado athletic director

At least somebody could see the lighter side:

"It's been a fun year for all of us. We got to see Notre Dame go from an academic institute to a banking institute."

—Joe Paterno

But methinks the protests of these athletic directors ring a little hollow. After all, if they were in Notre Dame's position, they'd probably do the same thing. Because they know, as do the good Jesuits of South Bend, that Mammon rules the college game just as certainly as it does the pros. And this leads us to our final question:

ISSUE NO. 7

Why all this praying and carrying on among players at the end of NFL games?

It's apparently the latest trend, even more popular than the run 'n' shoot. Players—often from both teams—hold hands and have a prayer session right there on the field after a game. Players say they're doing it as testimony to their faith in God.

"Personally, I think it's weak. I don't think your average fan goes to football games to be touched. I don't think that when he loads up the thermos and pays $10 to park, he's looking to get proselytized. . . . Sure, athletes are entitled to freedom of religion like anybody else. But let them exercise it on their own time."

—Rick Reilly, columnist

Speaking for myself, I've got nothing against people praying at football games or anywhere else. My only hope is that God isn't spending a lot of time watching NFL games. Because, you know, if that's the way He's spending his Sunday afternoons, sitting in front of the tube watching the Giants bash Atlanta, we're all in deep trouble.

"I had my own feelings about praying before a game. If God would just stay out of it, I would win it by myself."

—Bernie Parrish, Browns defensive back

14

The Stupor Bowl: An Unauthorized History of America's Most Over-Hyped Sporting Event and the Strange and Fascinating Personalities Who Have Made It What It Is Today

If it's the ultimate game, Duane Thomas asked once, why do they play it every year?

Good question. And some years it would've been better if they'd just held the parties and forgotten about the game.

"The first Super Bowl had uncertainty going for it. The third Super Bowl had Joe Namath going for it. The other Super Bowls have been Hackensack in the garbage burning season."
—Larry Merchant, columnist

"The Super Bowl is a day of national celebration when, for a few hours, nearly everyone in America puts aside his everyday concerns, gathers his family and friends 'round the big screen TV to watch—not eat—a turkey."
—Mike Littwin, columnist

Not all the games have been bad. Bills-Giants, 49ers-Bengals (the second one), Cowboys-Steelers, Steelers-Rams were all crackerjack football games. But so many Super Sundays have turned out to be duds or blowouts that it's almost become a joke. It's a little like a guy who takes a beautiful woman to bed and then falls asleep before doing what they came there to do. Lots of sweaty

Without Joe Namath, most Super Bowls have been "Hackensack in the garbage burning season."

anticipation, with no payoff in the end. That's the Super Bowl most years.

The game that put the Super Bowl on the map was III. Joe "I guarantee it!" Namath promised that his underdog Jets would beat the highly favored Colts, and damned if he didn't back up the pledge. Of course, if Joe had played for St. Louis or Minnesota or somebody like that, nobody in the media would have much cared what he said or did. But since he played for a New York team, and his remarks got blown up bigger than V-J Day, all the publicity helped turn a fine little sporting event into the over-stimulated quasi-national holiday that we have come to know and love.

In New York, fathers tell their sons of the time Joe encountered Lou Michaels in that Italian restaurant in Miami a few nights before the game. Michaels, the aging defensive end for Baltimore, was stuffing his face with pasta when in came Namath, styling in a full-length fur coat with babes on both arms. (The story keeps getting embellished over the years.) By then Namath's remarks predicting a win had been all over the papers, and Michaels stood up and said he didn't much like it.

> Michaels: "You're doing a lot of talking."
> Namath: "There's a lot to talk about."
> Michaels: "Haven't you ever heard of humility?"
> Namath: "We're going to beat you, and I'm gonna pick you apart."
> Michaels: "You're gonna find it tough throwing out of a well."
> Namath: "My blockers will give me time."
> Michaels: "Suppose we kick the hell out of you?"
> Namath: "I'll sit right down on the middle of the field and cry."

The only ones doing the crying after the game were Michaels and the Colts, and years later Michaels was still upset about the way Namath behaved:

"He was not a nice man at all. He was very egotistical. He bad-mouthed my friends, Unitas and Earl Morrall. If I were in his position, I'd have been a lot more humble. People tell me he's changed, but I don't believe that. I give him credit for that one game he had against us. Sure. But I'll tell you what. If we had beaten the Jets, nobody would know who Joe Namath is today."

Namath was a product, and emblem, of his time. Young, arrogant, rebellious. Fast-living, a swinger with the ladies. He is probably the most famous football player ever to play the game, and also one of the best. Although, before the Super Bowl, many football "experts" regarded him as an impostor.

But they don't make football coaches without flaws—God knows—and even St. Vince had his detractors:

"He never told Jim Taylor, one of his greatest players, that he was even a good ballplayer. Taylor wanted to hear it from his lips. To Lombardi, the team was Lombardi and Lombardi was the team."

—Larry Merchant

"I had great respect for Lombardi. But he was an emotional guy and I wasn't. He interpreted that as not taking my job seriously. My feeling about his pep talks was: Get it over with and let's get out of here and play. I don't need that bull."

—Steve Wright, who played four years under Lombardi

Before the first AFL-NFL World Championship Game—the "Super Bowl" tag had not yet been pinned on it—Lombardi showed thinly veiled contempt for the rival league and its champion, the Kansas City Chiefs. But Chiefs cornerback Fred "The Hammer" Williamson got a bunch of press for showing a lack of respect himself:

"I haven't seen anything in the films that offers much of a threat to me. I'll be able to cover either Boyd Dowler or Carroll Dale. . . . I guarantee you they won't beat me on a deep pattern. Dale has moves like Art Graham of Boston, and Dowler is like Glenn Bass of Buffalo. And Graham and Bass are not among the top receivers in our league. I'll just dump Dowler when he leaves the line of scrimmage. If he catches the ball, I'll drop the hammer on him. Two hammers on Dowler and one on Dale should be enough. Bart Starr. Who's he anyway?"

Williamson got his lip buttoned by Starr, who threw for a pair of touchdowns, and doddering old Max McGee, a little-used receiver who had thought so much of the Chiefs and his chances of playing that he had stayed out partying all night before the game. Then he got up and cleared his head enough to catch seven passes to help the Pack bury Kansas City, 35–10, and leave the Chiefs muttering in the locker room afterward:

"It's impossible for me to believe that those balding old men on the Packers could have handled us with such ridiculous ease."

—Jerry Mays, defensive lineman

But the Chiefs came back for Super Bowl IV and handled the Vikings as easily as the Packers had handled them. The unfortunate Vikes, losers of four Super Bowls in all, were quarterbacked by Joe Kapp, who was full of bluster and wobbly spirals. Though not blessed with a great arm or great speed, he was a scrambler and a fighter and a terrific competitor.

After passing for seven touchdowns in a game against Baltimore, tying an NFL record, Kapp stuck up eight fingers and shouted at the Colts:

"Shall we go for the record? Just hang around and keep screwing up like you've been doing!"

Kapp was a character, all right. He had the psychological makeup of a linebacker or a special teams player, not a quarterback. While leading the Vikings to a win over the Packers and with a broken left wrist in a cast, he said to the Green Bay defense, "You cruds. You can't even beat me when I've got one arm." In his first year in the league, he said across the line of scrimmage: "Screw you, Rams. You're not much. Here I come."

Nobody was quite sure what to make of Kapp, but one opponent thought he had him figured out.

"He's got a suicide complex. Or, at least, some weird thing going."

—Ken Kortas, Steelers tackle

Kapp tried to get his weird thing going against Lenny Dawson and the Chiefs, but it wasn't nearly weird enough and the Vikings were blown out. Coming after Joe Willie Namath's called shot the year before, the Kansas City win was another dagger to the heart of the reputation of the old NFL and ushered in a decade-long era of AFC domination led by those great Miami and Pittsburgh clubs.

Those Steelers were a bunch of hard-nosed mothas. Jack Lambert, Mean Joe Greene, L. C. Greenwood, Dwight White, Mel Blount and the rest of them. Lambert may have had his finest moment in Super Bowl X, when Pittsburgh's kicker, Roy Gerela, botched a field goal. After the ball went awry, Dallas safety Cliff Harris patted Gerela on the helmet and said, "Roy, you're the best player we've got on our team." Hearing this, a furious Lambert picked up Harris bodily and slammed him to the ground.

The Steelers and Cowboys met again in Super Bowl XIII, a

35–31 thriller enlivened by the pre-game chatter of Dallas linebacker Thomas "Hollywood" Henderson. True to his nickname, Hollywood kept the spotlight focused on himself with his caustic comments about the powerhouse Steelers:

"Look at their tight end Randy Grossman. He's a substitute. With Bernie Cunningham out, that little guy's gonna have trouble over there with me. He's the smallest guy I ever played against. Grossman's a backup tight end? I mean, he's the guy that comes in when everybody's dead. He's the last hope."

And Hollywood, on Jack Lambert:

"I don't care for Jack Lambert either. Why? 'Cause he makes more money than I do and 'cause he don't have no teeth. He's like Dracula. He should at least keep a mouthpiece in there or something. Count Lambert, that's what I call him."

And Hollywood captured a tiny piece of football immortality with his classic comment about Steelers quarterback Terry Bradshaw, a man who, earlier in his career, was known alternately as "Ozark Ike," "Dummy" and "Country Bumpkin." Said Henderson:

"Terry Bradshaw couldn't spell cat if you spotted him the 'c' and the 'a.' "

Asked for a response, Bradshaw said, "This isn't nuclear physics. It's a game. How smart do you have to be?" But after completing 17 of 30 passes for 317 yards and four TDs, Bradshaw had an even better reply: "Go ask Henderson if I was dumb today."

The next year, the Steelers were considered such a lock to win their fourth Super Bowl that most people thought the Rams shouldn't even bother to show up.

"There are ways to make Super Bowl XIV competitive. Put weights on the Steelers. Make Terry Bradshaw throw left-handed. Let the Rams play with twelve men. Then it might be a game."

—Bob Rubin, sportswriter

The Rams had beaten lightly regarded Tampa Bay in the NFC Championship game—"a game for losers, played by losers," said one magazine writer—and were installed as heavy underdogs by Jimmy the Greek, the oddsmaker-commentator later fired by CBS for his slave-trader theories on racial evolution. The Ram players, however, thought the odds were way off.

"It's great for fans, bettors and neurotics to sit around and hypothesize about football games. I don't know where Jimmy the Greek gets his dope; but I can just see him in the prone position, with the telephone in his ear, getting his info. He doesn't look at movies; he doesn't talk to players. The line doesn't mean anything."

—Fred Dryer, defensive end

As is usually the case, the experts were proven wrong and the Rams, though losing, played the Steelers much tighter than anyone expected. That was Pittsburgh's fourth, and so far last, Super Bowl title, and since then we've come to know more about the interpersonal dynamics of that team, particularly as it concerned its star quarterback and coach Chuck Noll.

After retiring, Bradshaw called Noll "a jerk" and said that "perhaps it's a miracle we ever went to the Super Bowl, let alone won four of them," because they got along so poorly. Things really soured between the two in 1983 when Bradshaw hurt his elbow and played only one game. Recalls Terry:

"When I was injured late in my career, feeling insecure, unwanted and unneeded as a pro football player, like all injured players do, I felt Chuck was turning his back on me. When the end came, I needed Chuck most of all and he wasn't there."

Poor Terry. His feelings are always getting hurt. Like when he was elected to the Hall of Fame and the press needled him for picking his television partner, Verne Lundquist, to be his presenter rather than somebody from his old team. Said Terry, to the media assembled at Canton for the swearing-in ceremonies:

"It's the greatest day of my life, and I get nailed down here. What's with you people? My choice is very simple. For all you Pittsburghers, listen one more time and see if you all can't get this through your head . . ."

Bradshaw went on to explain that the man he felt closest to on the Steelers, former owner Art Rooney, was dead and thus unable to attend the ceremonies. "And I'm the type of person, in an event like this, that I'm not going to have some athlete or coach present me who I'm not going to see ever again." So he picked Verne.

Bradshaw was a truly great quarterback, the second best in Super Bowl history, but it should be pointed out that a person need not be extraordinarily gifted to play on a Super Bowl team. Look at Cliff Stoudt or Don Strock.

"A man named Cliff Stoudt has two Super Bowl rings from the Pittsburgh Steelers for doing nothing more strenuous than standing on the sideline keeping Terry Bradshaw's toupee dry. . . . [And] Don Strock backed up three different Super Bowl quarterbacks for Miami; he stood right beside Don Shula for so long people thought they'd been surgically bonded."
—Tony Kornheiser, *Washington Post*

Tom Landry coached in five Super Bowls and won two of them. A football icon nearly on the order of St. Vincent of Green Bay, he was so pious that in his early years he was known as Pope Landry I. As somber and stone-faced as a cigar store Indian, Landry was another coach who had problems with his star quarterback. In this case the quarterback was Don Meredith, who once said about Landry:

"He's a cold man, with no human understanding in him."

And, in a somewhat lighter vein:

"He's a perfectionist. If he was married to Raquel Welch, he'd expect her to cook."

Meredith was far more outgoing and expressive than his coach. Then again, a corpse was more outgoing than Landry. Nevertheless, in the seventies Old Stoneface built what came to be known as "America's Team."

"The Cowboys are like a woman who's had a lot of face-lifts. They're a fantasy from their uniforms to their stadium, which is like being in a living room. They have this holier-than-thou attitude that makes me sick."
—Howie Long, Raiders defensive lineman

Say what you will about them, the Cowboys had the greatest cheerleaders known to man and made their mark in Super Bowl lore with such players as the aforementioned Hollywood Henderson and Duane Thomas, who talked as little as Hollywood talked a lot. In time, though, Landry's holy water apparently got diluted and the Cowboys started to play like hell.

By the late eighties, even Tex Schramm, the longtime Dallas GM, was criticizing the coach:

"Some of the things we're doing are frankly mystifying. It's very seldom I put myself in the position of giving the players a reason for losing, but I'm not sure it's all on the players. We're having a lot of wins and losses that are difficult to accept. . . . We had an outstanding opportunity to get our team going Sunday. It was a terrible failure."

Schramm was not, however, referring to the game in 1988 when Landry, losing track of his team's field position, called the wrong play and cost the Cowboys the game. This prompted howls from the press:

"Landry routinely mispronounces players' names (Hogenbaum, Jethcoat), confuses teams (Oakland, Baltimore), but he usually knows where the ball is."

—Gary Myers, *Dallas Morning News*

Eventually Landry's head fell in a coup by new ownership, and the Pope's reputation took a terrible beating upon the publication of a book by Texas sportswriter Skip Bayless. The book contained allegations that Landry was a cold man with no human understanding who wanted Raquel Welch to cook and who mispronounced names, confused teams and did mystifying things. Mike Ditka, who caught a touchdown pass for the Cowboys in Super Bowl VI, disputed this characterization of his former coach and said so:

"Skip Bayless to me is a piss-ant that somebody should have stepped on a long time ago. People give you this bullcrap over Landry being plastic. I've watched the guy shed many a tear over cutting a player. . . . I happen to love him for the chance he gave me to get into and stay in the business I love."

As coach, Landry participated in one of the most memorable Super Bowls ever, the so-called "Blooper Bowl." Normally in Super Bowl competition—particularly if Denver or Minnesota is playing—one of the teams plays lousy and that's what turns the game into a turkey. But what made Super Bowl V so memorable was that both Dallas and Baltimore played like Peanut League teams. *Bad* Peanut League teams. The Colts fumbled five times and threw three interceptions and still won the game. Even the President of the United States, Richard Nixon, was given to comment, "I hope I don't make that many mistakes in one day."

Hate to tell you, Dick, but you did. And they were a lot worse than coughing up the pigskin inside the other team's 20. But that's beside the point. And the point is that Nixon was not only a diehard football fanatic—

"Nor is it an accident that the most repressive political regime in the history of this country is ruled by a football freak, Richard M. Nixon."

—Dave Meggysey, ex-football player

But that he also factored into Super Bowl history, albeit in a minuscule way. In 1972, the year after the Blooper Bowl, Nixon called Don Shula to suggest a play that the Dolphins could use when they met the Cowboys in Super Bowl VI. The president thought Paul Warfield could get open on down-and-in patterns over the middle. He was wrong. The Dolphins got creamed.

Nonetheless, the president's participation in the game is but one more piece of evidence that the Super Bowl is not a game at all. Not merely, anyway. Fran Tarkenton, who may be embittered because of the way he and the Vikings were treated at them, has described the annual Super Bowl bacchanalia as "a crass example of money ruining the purity of sport." And: "A manufactured megabucks extravaganza with lousy play [that] has sold out to the dollar."

It *is* a monument to excess, American style. Fiddle-playing Nero would have been happy as a clam during Super Bowl week in New Orleans. So what's wrong with that? And another thing about it, it has Roman numerals.

"This is a particularly ingenious invention, as they seem to lend historical importance to a simple game of football. Super Bowl 24. There it is in print with the more familiar Arabic numbers. Written this way, it certainly seems less like a monumental event, and more like something from the inventory list of a plumbing supply house."

—Robert Klein, comedian

What helps create, and in turn feeds on, the excesses of the Super Bowl are the media. More media people than Hannibal had elephants descend on the game every year, posing the same questions over and over to the overwhelmed participants.

"If you were filming sharks feeding, this is as close as you would get. . . . It's like having a root canal for the players."

—Joe Theismann, former Super Bowl quarterback for the Redskins, on "Media Day"

Manny Fernandez, who played in the Super Bowl with the Dolphins, uses the same dental analogy to explain the endless interviews that players must endure: "It's like going to the dentist every day to have the same tooth filled." Ouch!

Hunter Thompson, he of "Gonzo journalism" fame, attended Super Bowl VIII at Houston in 1974, and explains what it was like to be a reporter there:

"I remember being shocked at the sloth and moral degeneracy of the Nixon press corps during the 1972 presidential campaign. But they were like a pack of wolverines on speed compared to the relatively elite sportswriters who showed up in Houston to cover the Super Bowl. For eight long and degrading days, I skulked around with all the other professionals, doing our jobs—which was actually to do nothing except drink all the free booze we could pour into our bodies, courtesy of the National Football League, and listen to some of the lamest and silliest swill ever uttered by man or beast."

It takes a certain type of individual to flourish in an atmosphere such as this. The old Oakland Raiders had a bunch of them—guys like John Matuszak and Lyle Alzado and the sweet-talking Lester Hayes. They roamed around the bars of Bourbon Street in 1981 while Dick Vermeil's Philadelphia Eagles stayed in their rooms and studied their playbooks like good Boy Scouts. The Boy Scouts got stomped.

A personal favorite of mine from those old Oakland Raider days was Otis Sistrunk, a bald-headed defensive lineman with a fearsome visage:

"Otis Sistrunk was so ugly that he could hurt you just by looking at you."

—A fan

"That's Otis Sistrunk. He's from the University of Mars."
—Alex Karras, *Monday Night Football* announcer, as the camera focused in on Sistrunk standing on the sidelines without his helmet on

The Raiders won it all again in 1984, and although by then the team had moved to Los Angeles, the team retained the old Oakland way of doing things. Matt Millen describes what it was like:

"Howie Long would be running around the locker room. Lyle Alzado would try to bite guys. Then John Matuszak would come over and yell, 'I'm sane! I'm sane!' "

Nor did the Raiders—when they were still in Oakland—much appreciate the rising power across the bay, the San Francisco 49ers. Said Millen:

"When I was with the Raiders in Oakland, we always hated Dwight Clark, because he was so pretty, and [Joe] Montana because he was so good. We were your basic, subhuman group—you know, dragging your knuckles on the ground. They were the clean cut guys."

As it turned out, those clean-cut guys could sure play football. The 49ers' first of four Super Bowl titles came in 1982. Back then many of its stars—Clark, Montana, Ronnie Lott—were not well known and the team itself was considered suspect. Before their NFC championship game against Dallas, Ed "Too Tall" Jones of the Cowboys said that he didn't have much respect for the 49ers and didn't know many of their names.

The 49ers said nothing in response, though they obviously read Too Tall's remarks in the paper. At one point Montana ran a bootleg around Jones's side. Too Tall was the only player who could stop him, and Montana gave him a fake and ran for 30 yards. As Montana came back to the huddle, jogging past Jones, he hissed,

"Respect that, motherfucker."

Particularly when he was young and had something to prove, Montana was a firecracker of a quarterback who could get up in your face and stay there. He would not let up on Too Tall, who had also criticized the 49ers' long passing game, saying that Montana could not throw deep. After completing a long pass deep into Cowboy territory, Joe again accosted Too Tall, saying,

"Is that long enough for you, you SOB?"

Finally, it came down to Montana scrambling away from Jones and Harvey Martin with seconds left in the game. As Montana let go of the ball, Jones and Martin smashed him to the ground. In the end zone Dwight Clark was leaping high to make "The Catch," and the Cowboys were losers.

"You've just beaten America's Team," said a dazed Martin.

And Montana, picking himself up, replied, "Well, you can just sit home with the rest of America and watch the Super Bowl."

The 49ers beat the Bengals in Super Bowl XVI, then in 1984 whipped the Dolphins. Before the game many experts thought the Dolphins were the superior team, but the Miami defense turned out to be a fraud.

"After looking at the films, we said, 'This is a Super Bowl defense?' "

—49ers line coach Bob McKittrick, preparing to play the Dolphins in Super Bowl XIX

The same thing could have been asked about New England's defense, which was buried the following year by the Bears, 46–10, in Super Bowl XX. One Chicago fan's button said it all: "WE CAME. WE SAW. WE KICKED ASS."

Super Bowl XX was everything we've come to expect from a Super Bowl: huge hyped-up Super Week extravaganza, followed by a lousy game. But at least XX offered some diversion, a real wise guy in the tradition of a Joe Namath or a Hollywood Henderson. His name: Jim McMahon.

In protest against not being allowed to wear a commercial headband of his choosing, McMahon wore a headband that said "Rozelle" on it. He wore sunglasses indoors. One story quoted him as saying that New Orleans women were "sluts." This report proved to be false, but it drove women office workers to picket the team hotel demanding McMahon's head. Instead he offered something else. He mooned a helicopter passing over the practice field. And he demanded that the Bears fly his personal acupuncturist out to New Orleans to treat his sore behind. Even if he hadn't played in the game at all, McMahon would have had a pretty decent week.

McMahon had his act working well before the Super Bowl, of course. He was the best-known personality on America's best football team, a team with a rosterful of headline-hoggers, Mike Ditka, Refrigerator Perry and Buddy Ryan among them. He wore an earring and dressed in leopard pants when he met the press. He played golf in his bare feet and delighted in flouting traditionalists of every stripe.

One of his targets was Doug Flutie, whom McMahon often referred to as "Bambi, America's favorite midget." The Boston College whiz kid came to the Bears in 1986, after their Super Bowl season, and McMahon and some others made no secret of their dislike for the rookie. (Dan Hampton called him "that fawn-like creature.")

Flutie quarterbacked the Bears in their losing 1987 playoff game against the Redskins, while McMahon tended an injured shoulder on the sidelines. The next season Flutie was gone and McMahon was back as quarterback of the Bears, though still nursing a grudge against the little fellow:

"I don't have anything against Doug Flutie as a person. What I said when he came here, I still stand by. I didn't think we needed him at the time and since then, we let him go, so how important was he to our team?"

Playing in the 1988 playoffs, against Washington, McMahon was asked how he thought the Bears would fare with him at quarterback as opposed to Flutie the previous year. McMahon responded:

"I think we've grown a little, so we should be higher for this game than we were last year, or at least taller. Just say we'll be head and shoulders above where we were a year ago at quarterback. Maybe a belly button too."

A lot of people thought McMahon was funny. A lot of people did not. Those who did not had themselves a good laugh when, like Flutie before him, McMahon was deemed an expendable commodity and shipped off to the Chargers before the 1989 season. Some opinions from the press at the time:

"The Bears are better off losing with somebody else at quarterback than winning with a boorish lout. . . . We should be thankful the deal was announced on a Friday so we can celebrate all weekend."

—Mike Imrem, *Arlington* (Illinois) *Daily Herald*

"The trade was necessary because under no circumstances would McMahon have willingly accepted his role of backup. McMahon is one of the most overrated quarterbacks of this generation."

—Terry Boers, *Chicago Sun-Times*

"It is a trade that had to be made, like a boil that has to be lanced. Were the personalities different, the Bears quarterback situation would have been ideal, youth reinforced by experience.

Jim McMahon mooned a helicopter at a Super Bowl practice. Observers in the helicopter reported later that they were not sure whether they were seeing McMahon's bottom or his face.

But McMahon was too divisive and Ditka too vindictive to make it work."

—Bernie Lincicome, *Chicago Tribune*

In San Diego, McMahon took a few parting shots of his own, comparing Willie Gault of the Bears unfavorably with the Charger receivers he was now working with:

"Not only do the receivers have great speed, but they have great hands. That's something I wasn't accustomed to in Chicago. We had a speed burner, but he didn't catch the ball all that well. I don't see anybody out here with boxing gloves on."

And get this: McMahon said that the reason he had to leave the Bears was that *Ditka's* ego was too big . . .

"You know Mike's ego. Anybody who can take away his spotlight, he's going to get rid of. Mike believes he can get it done with anybody. His coaching gets it done."

We'll let the football fans of America decide who was right— Ditka or McMahon—but Mike Lupica's assessment of Jimbo after he left the Bears does seem to have possessed uncanny foresight:

"In about five years McMahon will have to hijack a plane to get his name in the newspapers."

The Redskins won two Super Bowls in the decade—the first dominated by John "Reagan may be president, but today I'm king" Riggins, and the second by a somewhat more poignant figure, Doug Williams.

Williams was the first and so far only black man to quarterback a Super Bowl champion. He led the 'Skins' rampage over the hapless Denver Broncos, but almost as soon as he got to the top of the mountain, he fell off. Injuries took their toll over the next couple of seasons, and he played only sparingly. Two years after quarterbacking them to the Super Bowl title, the Redskins Plan B'd him and when no other teams would take a chance on him, they let him go.

Coach Joe Gibbs said the Redskins were going with a youth movement, but shortly after dumping Williams they signed a 33-year-old nobody by the name of Jeff Rutledge. Williams is still bitter about this, saying,

"Joe lied to me. Don't tell me you're going with a youth movement and sign Rutledge. Don't tell me you can't bear to see me as a backup."

The Redskins have said they doubted Williams could adjust as a backup, but Doug disputes this:

"Joe has a short memory. When he says it has to do with my back, he forgets that he played me eight weeks after back surgery. He didn't worry about my health at that point."

Another star for the Redskins in Super Bowl XXII, running back Timmy Smith, has accused general manager Bobby Beathard of blackballing him around the league with rumors about drugs and an alleged lack of discipline. Smith was let go by the Redskins a year after XXII and, after brief stints with the Cowboys and Chargers, is now out of football. Beathard is now GM of San Diego, and he hotly denies the accusation.

"Players blackball themselves. It's easy to use somebody else as an excuse. Dan Henning [San Diego coach] and [Dallas coach] Jimmy Johnson wanted to give him a fresh start. If he's a good player and can help a team, nobody is going to listen to me. The Cowboys didn't ask me once about Timmy Smith. Timmy is his own worst enemy."

It's true that Super Bowl heroes do not fare as well as they might hope after the cheering stops. When the 49ers won their third one in 1989, after beating the hard-luck Bengals with a station-to-station drive in the final minutes, wide receiver Jerry Rice was named MVP. But Rice pouted afterward that he was not getting the recognition from the media he deserved and implied that the reason for this was that he is black.

"[I'm] not getting my name out there. I don't know if I'll get any recognition in commercials or anything, but right now, the way things are looking, I'm not going to get nothing out of being the MVP. I really don't want all the recognition, but I feel like I deserve to get some of it. If it were Joe Montana or Dwight Clark, there would have been headlines all over."

Rice complained that as MVP he, not Montana, should have been the one to say, "I'm going to Disney World!" to the cameras after the game. But Disney World pointed out that Doug Williams had gotten to say the magic words after he led the Redskins to victory in Super Bowl the year before, and that it was the amusement park's long-standing policy to have only quarterbacks as spokesmen. Many in the media also didn't think Rice was being shut out as he claimed. Among other things, he appeared on the cover of *Sports Illustrated* after the game and his picture was spread all over Bay Area newspapers.

"Folks, if this is an example of being snubbed by the media, then we should all be so lucky! [Rice's complaint] trivializes genu-

Jerry Rice won the Super Bowl MVP, but whined when he didn't get to go to Disney World.

ine racist issues and hurts the cause of someone who has genuine discrimination complaints."

—John Dvorak, San Francisco columnist

"Why was Rice complaining in the first place? Aren't athletes, purportedly as modest as he, supposed to be indifferent to head-lines? Don't the real rewards come in the form of respect from their peers? That, at any rate, is what they keep telling us. So why does Rice want his 'name out there'? He gave us the answer himself: He wants those television commercials. He wants to go out and sell Japanese cars, after-shave lotion and office furniture on the old tube because that's where the real dough is. The modern athlete doesn't play for *la gloire* or even a healthy paycheck; he plays to become a television huckster."

—Ron Fimrite, *Sports Illustrated*

But let's not leave this abbreviated Super Bowl history on a sour note. The Silver Anniversary game between the Giants and the Bills was a corker after all, one of the best ever. For Bill Parcells and the Giants it was their second Super Bowl title in four years. Their first one came in 1987, and lots of football fans were happy to see that season end if for no other reason than they didn't want to see another damned bucket of Gatorade dumped over Parcells's head.

New York book publishers apparently couldn't get enough of that Gatorade routine, though.

"Studies show that 96 percent of the books published in America are ghostwritten autobiographies of New York athletes. When the Giants won the Super Bowl, they inspired a greater outpouring of literature than did the Third Reich, rising and falling."

—Scott Ostler, columnist

Giants players (and their ghostwriters) produced 11 books after their Super Bowl win. In fact, they did a lot better in publishing books than they did winning games the next season.

"Who would have thought the New York Giants would produce more books than victories in 1987?"

—Jim Donaldson, reporter

Time will tell how many books the Giants will produce after Super Bowl Win No. 2, but the New York players, if not Publishing Row, seem to have gotten this whole Super Bowl business into the proper perspective. As Lawrence Taylor, an avid golfer, puts it:

"I'd rather go to the Super Bowl than shoot 70, but I'd rather shoot 65 than play in the Super Bowl."

15

The Rooting Interest: What Players and Coaches Really Think of Us, the Loyal Fans

One of the more heartwarming aspects of professional football is the unflagging respect that players, coaches and owners have for the men and women who watch their games.

"A typical fan is a guy who sits on the 40, criticizes the coaches and the players and has all the answers. Then he leaves the stadium and can't find his car."
—Dennis Erickson, upwardly aspiring college coach

The fans buy the tickets, they go to the games, and they root for the home team. They care passionately about their teams, and they cheer them on from coast to coast.

"Down there, you're tied 17–17 in the middle of the third quarter with one team driving for the go-ahead score. Then someone hollers, 'Surf's up!' and that's it. Everyone leaves the stadium."
—Matt Millen, on playing in Los Angeles

"You try running a shotgun in New Orleans or Minnesota, and see how far you get. Our fans come in, and I'm surprised they don't serve bullion or a little chicken soup to keep the other guys warm while they're playing."
—Bill Parcells, complaining about the quiet New York crowds during a recent Giants season

Well, even if some fans don't cheer as loudly as they could, the players always want to see them turn out for the game anyway.

"I'll tell you what I think of Namath after his first pro game."
—Norm Van Brocklin, when asked his opinion of
Namath prior to the game against the Colts

This was in 1969, before the NFL and AFL merged, and there
was genuine animosity between the leagues. Players and coaches
in the NFL regarded themselves as the biggest and the baddest on
the block, and the AFL resented the hell out of this. They thought
they played football on a par with the NFL, and in the outspoken
Namath, they found themselves a champion. Asked about Earl
Morrall, the quarterback for the Colts, Joe said,

"I can think of five quarterbacks in the AFL better than Morrall. Myself, John Hadl of San Diego, Bob Griese of Miami,
Daryle Lamonica of Oakland, and Len Dawson of Kansas City."

People warned that such statements by Namath, including his
"guarantee" the Jets were going to win, were going to rile up the
Colts and inspire them to victory. But Joe was unconcerned:

"They say the Colts are going to take my statement and put
it up on their bulletin board. Psychologically, it's going to lift them
up for the game. If the Colts need anything like that to lift them
up for the game, then they're in trouble from the beginning."

Besides beating the Colts 16–7, what Namath and the Jets did
was knock the stuffing out of the pompous windbags of the NFL
and their self-righteous claims of superiority. The NFL's attitude
stemmed in large part from the first two Super Bowl contests in
which the Chiefs and Raiders were struck down by the almighty
Green Bay Packers and their coach Vince Lombardi, or "St.
Vince," as some called him.

"Vince didn't like the courses in religion we took, so he created
his own religion."
—A teammate of Lombardi's at Fordham
University, where Lombardi went to college

Lombardi's religion was football. And he cast such an aura
that, even today, those who knew him speak in worshipful tones
about the man. He was pious, stern, lordly. Compared to him
Moses was a wallflower. The story goes that Lombardi and his
wife were in bed one night. "God, your feet are cold," Mrs.
Lombardi complained. Lombardi replied: "You may call me Vincent, dear."

"Most of the people come here to bad-mouth us anyway. We've got enough people doing that. As far as I'm concerned they can stay home."
—Irving Fryar, wide receiver, commenting on the small crowds attending Patriot games

But what is universal around the league is the high opinion that players and coaches have for the observations of the men and women sitting in the seats of the stadium or watching at home.

"Let 'em say what they're going to say. I say he's gonna make it. When this season's over, I'm gonna walk down Michigan Boulevard and I'm gonna take my pants down and there's one million guys that's gonna have to come over and kiss my ass."
—Abe Gibron, Bears coach, defending his choice of starting quarterback against criticism by fans

"These fans don't understand. They call pro football a game. It isn't a game. Playing Scrabble, playing dice, those are games. You don't break your neck playing Scrabble."
—Eric Dickerson, running back

It's the inalienable right of every fan to boo. Players know this, and they accept it.

"I never knew they were booing me. But now that you tell me, to hell with them."
—Craig Heyward, Saints running back, after he was booed during a game

"I can deal with the fans. They're a bunch of kiss-asses anyway. If that's the worst thing that's going to happen in life, I'll accept it and go on."
—Mike Tomczak, Bears quarterback, after being booed by Chicago fans when he was shaken up on a play

It's true that some people can be front-runners, but the real fans stick with a team through thick and thin.

"Why don't those people go hide in their closets? They're taking the easy way out. If we lose, we lose, but I'd hate to be stuck in a closet."
—John Elway, responding to comments by some Denver fans that they didn't want to see the Broncos

> play against the 49ers in Super Bowl XXIV, for fear
> they'd be crushed again. (They were.)

Real fans stick with their team when things get tough, and when they get very cold, real fans paint their chests and take off their shirts.

> "Look at those guys. They must be mentally retarded. I bet their parents were cousins."
>
> —Canadian football executive, observing some shirtless football fans cavorting in sub-freezing temperatures

Okay, it's true. Not all coaches appreciate the comments of fans. Not all players respect the fan's right to boo. And not all owners think that the antics of their ticket-paying customers are always charming.

But, to a man, all the coaches, players and owners agree that it is the fans who make professional football the great game it is today. It is, after all, the ticket-buying, product-purchasing, television-watching public that makes the game such a highly profitable one for the NFL, and because of this, people all across America deserve a large vote of thanks.

> "I don't care about those people up there. Those guys have got to get up and go to work in the morning at about 6 o'clock. I have the day off tomorrow, and I might just go to the bank and count my money."
>
> —Neon Deion Sanders, cornerback

16

The Fifth Quarter: A Random Assortment of Cheap Shots, Low Blows, Rude Remarks and Provocative Thoughts That Wouldn't Fit Anywhere Else

"Dick Butkus is an animal. He doesn't shower after a game. He licks himself clean."
> —Alex Hawkins, on the Hall of Fame linebacker

"I didn't see that he had anything to be proud of."
> —Buddy Ryan, after watching a streaker who ran across the field during a game

"Look at all the women that go get married to older men or rich men and stay married for a couple months or a year and, boom, they're out and they want $10 million or $20 million because they feel like they've had mental cruelty. How in the world can a woman say she deserves half of what I have because she stayed married to me for two years? She's never carried a football, she's never been hit once, or played with a hurt hamstring."
> —The ever-enlightened Eric Dickerson, explaining why he's avoiding marriage

"Joe Ferguson may be 40, but he's got the body of a 39-year-old."
> —TV commentator Paul Maguire, on the backup quarterback

"Barry Manilow looks like you do when you see your face in the reflection in the bathroom faucet."
> —Lineman Curt Marsh, on hearing that Manilow would sing the National Anthem before a game

"That probably gave new meaning to the phrase 'pigskin.'"
> —Reporter Charles Jeffries, on hearing that Roseanne Barr had mooned the crowd at a college football game

"I know one thing's for sure. Talent is a lot of bullshit. When you hear somebody ask, 'What kind of football player is he?' and the answer is, 'Well, he has talent,' what they're really saying is he isn't worth a crap yet."
> —Jim Burt, nose tackle

"It gets down to this. To win you must have athletes. To have athletes you must break the rules. There's not a team in the top 20 that doesn't cheat in some way."
> —Harry Edwards, UC Berkeley professor, on the secret of success in college football

"I just don't like indoor domes. They just weren't meant for football. It's unfortunate people spend a lot of money building them. Domes should be used for roller rinks."
> —Mike Ditka

"We're in the driver's seat now. The Rams—they're parking cars."
> —Raiders running back Greg Bell, on his old team, the Los Angeles Rams

"Waiting for the Rams to win a Super Bowl is like leaving the porch light on for Jimmy Hoffa."
> —Milton Berle, comic

"What do Jimmy Swaggart and Saints coach Jim Mora have in common? They can get 60,000 people under one roof screaming, 'Jesus Christ.'"
> —Steven Brier, reporter

"If their IQs were five points lower, they'd be geraniums."
> —Tight end Russ Francis, on defensive linemen

"The Raiders' Jay Schroeder was intercepted so many times on Sunday that he's got a new nickname—Scud."
> —Bob Dorfman, reporter

"He looks like a professional blood donor. He makes Lou Holtz healthy."

—Tony Kornheiser, on emaciated Seahawks coach Chuck Knox after a diet

"We definitely will be improved this year. Last year we lost 10 games. This year we only scheduled nine."

—Ray Jenkins, old-time Montana State football coach

"We were flat as a plate of piss."

—Former Giants coach Joe Schmidt, after his team lost a game (Schmidt is also responsible for the famous maxim: "Life is a shit sandwich and every day you take a bite.")

"The only time Jimmy didn't run up a score was 27 years ago when he took the SAT."

—Broadcaster Jim Nantz, on Cowboys coach Jimmy Johnson

"The MVP in the Super Bowl doesn't mean a hill of beans. It's just winning the game. Who cares who the MVP is? Just win the game. That's all that matters."

—Terry Bradshaw, former Super Bowl MVP

"Some of the players are good. There's a bigger bunch that ain't."

—F. G. Hocutt, longtime Alabama fan, assessing a recent Crimson Tide football roster

"New Orleans is a tough place. One thing I would say is, I don't think it's a very good place for children and families. There's not a lot for kids to do."

—Broncos owner Pat Bowlen, sizing up the host city for Super Bowl XXIV, New Orleans, in remarks that caused a civic controversy

"Gaston Green plays so sparingly and dresses so smartly that he might consider coming out with his own line of inactive wear."

—Sportswriter Chris Dufresne, on the Rams non-running back

"We were tipping off our plays. Whenever we broke from the huddle, three backs were laughing and one was as pale as a ghost."

—Former Oilers GM John Breen, on a woeful Houston club

"Dwight Clark tells everybody who asks, and some who don't, that he wants to be a general manager, but 49ers fans better hope that it's for another team. Nice guy Dwight is great at working with the public, but I doubt that he has the depth of intellect or the perseverance to be a success as a general manager."
—Columnist Glenn Dickey, on the
receiver-turned-49ers front office man

"I thought maybe I was going to become a general manager, because I kept wanting to take a nap."
—Jerry Glanville, describing a recent
bout with pneumonia

"When they go into a restaurant, they don't look at a menu. They get an estimate."
—Sportscaster Steve Alvarez,
on some beefy Ohio State linemen

Question: "How can Roger Craig gain 50 yards in a game?"
Answer: "Give him the ball 50 times."
—Joke about the former 49ers running back in his
last year with the team

"If someone did that when I played, his own teammates would have strangled him. It's childish and unprofessional. If I want to watch somebody act like they're sick with St. Vitus's dance, I'll go to the movies."
—Ex-NFL tackle Art Donovan, on end zone dances

"Tell him to give me back my clothes. He's the cheapest guy I've ever met. Half the clothes he has, he got from me."
—Raiders lineman Howie Long, on Matt Millen
after Millen was traded from LA to the 49ers

"I have seen guys look happier throwing up."
—Columnist Jim Murray, on the game face of
former Chargers coach Don Coryell

"The only thing that will turn around the Patriots is if they get better players. And who now holds the ultimate authority over player personnel? A 56-year-old guy who has no NFL experience . . . Aren't you impressed? Owner Victor Kiam is going to pay Jankovich about $2.5 million over the next five years, and Jankovich may not know if player-personnel director Joe Mendes is picking the next Marcus Allen or Woody Allen."

—Columnist Alan Greenberg, on the hiring of Sam
Jankovich as GM of New England

"Those who can, do; those who can't, teach; those who can't teach, teach gym; those who can't teach gym, work color for ABC Sports."

—Norman Chad, TV critic

"Interviewing naked or half-naked athletes in a locker room—for men or women—might be the foulest chore in journalism, other than working for *USA Today.*"

—More media criticism from Norman Chad

"Splash some on, you chew gum like a cow."

—Columnist Mitch Albom,
on a new Mike Ditka cologne

"The whole story is about one vindictive person who wants to rub the system in your nose and jam it down your throat. He's punishing him. He's playing big shot. Jim Finks is a power freak. It's a shame that much power is in one person's hands, but he'll pay for it."

—Player agent Greg Campbell, representing
quarterback Bobby Hebert, discussing Saints
president Jim Finks

"I felt like a kid in a candy store. You walk in there and nobody's stopping you. It was like playing catch."

—Rams receiver Henry Ellard, after a 12-catch
game against the Colts

"We're not shooting ourselves in the foot. We're actually amputating both legs."

—Ron Meyer, Colts coach

"The NFL has no right issuing fines to Jerry Glanville or any other coach who pops off in public. So Glanville called Jack Pardee 'a jerk.' So what? He can say whatever he likes. Good heavens, it's nice to hear someone being honest for a change. Most coaches would have said, 'We have every reason to believe Pardee is a jerk, but at this point in time, we have to look at the films.' "

—Bruce Jenkins, columnist

"We seem to attract our own."
—Steelers coach Chuck Noll, after a sewer pipe
broke and spilled into the Pittsburgh locker room
after a bad loss

"He thinks I'm arrogant, and he tried to belittle my work. I
didn't try to antagonize him, but he took everything I said wrong.
It's difficult to have a personality conflict with someone who
doesn't have a personality."
—Lon Simmons, on the man who fired him as 49ers
radio announcer, Mickey Luckoff

"What do I need spies for? I know what they're working on.
They've only got four running plays."
—Giants coach Bill Parcells, after being accused of
planting a spy to watch the Redskins practice

"When people in Green Bay say they have a nice wardrobe, it
means they have 10 bowling shirts."
—Greg Koch, Dolphins tackle (After this remark a
pair of Wisconsin deejays sent Koch over 100
bowling shirts, a bowling ball and a note that read:
"Dear Greg. Take a fashion risk. Wear one of these
and jump off a cliff.")

"We'd hand them a caramel candy, and if they took the wrap-
per off before they ate it, they'd get a basketball scholarship. If
they ate the caramel with the paper still on it, we'd give them a
football scholarship."
—Basketball coach Frank Layden, on the recruiting
techniques at Niagara University

"For years, the Bengals drafted kids that looked like Tarzan,
and played like Jane."
—Cris Collinsworth, on his former team

"Getting replaced by Bill Curry, that really bothered me. It's
kind of like having your wife run off with Don Knotts."
—Pepper Rodgers, after being replaced as head
coach of Georgia Tech by Curry

"Sure I would. I'd miss him too."
—Arkansas athletic director Frank Broyles, asked if
he'd still like the Razorback football coach if they
lost half their games

"The Bengals beat the awful Cleveland Browns on Monday night and Sam Wyche makes it sound as if the Bengals had successfully landed on the beach at Normandy. So now Sam sounds just as unusual talking about football as he does talking about everything else."

—Mike Lupica, columnist

"I think guys who don't come to camp should be tied to a trailer hitch and drug around Fulton County."

—Jerry Glanville, after a Falcon player reported late
to training camp following a holdout

"When Fred Akers was in Texas, they never had to send the steers to the slaughterhouse. He just bored them to death."

—Columnist Terry Boers,
on the former Longhorns coach

"Joe Kapp seems intent on becoming the southbound horse's north end of the year by acclamation."

—Columnist Kent Gilchrist, after Kapp was fired as
GM of the British Columbia Lions of Canadian football

"It's an animal game. I'm an animal. Any guy good at it is an animal. Is it normal to wake up in the morning in a sweat because you can't wait to beat another human's guts out?"

—Joe Kapp, when he was a player

"You hear it over and over again, how their offense is so unstoppable. Their coach, Jenkins, has been talking a lot of smack in the papers about what they did to us last year and two years ago. Well, this is 1990, and it feels good to make them shut their mouths."

—Texas cornerback Willie Mack Garza, after the
Longhorns whipped John Jenkins's Cougars

"The NFL must get rid of artificial turf. Whatever it takes, get rid of the stuff. Any football player who doesn't want the stuff ripped up is a fool."

—Dave Kindred, columnist

"Anthony—You were great, but your teammates stunk."

—Monita Carter, Anthony's mom, after watching
her son catch four passes in a bad Viking
loss to the Dolphins

"Bernie Kosar's right arm has digressed from grandfatherly to D.O.A."

—Mark Heisler, on the Browns quarterback

"GO BRAVES—AND TAKE THE FALCONS WITH YOU."

—Atlanta bumper sticker

"It doesn't much matter whether the NCAA stands for Nerds, Clods and Androids, or Nitwits, Clowns and Assholes. They all fit."

—Dan Jenkins, writer

"I mean, when the Chiefs score a measly field goal, it's a sideline spectacle. Kicker Nick Lowery hugs everyone except Lamar Hunt after each three-pointer. Nick gets more hugs after a field goal than Marge Schott got after the World Series."

—Tom Friend, columnist

"I detest Little League baseball and youth football. No matter how they piously pledge otherwise, too many coaches who run those teams apply terrific pressure to win before kids are ready. For every kid who feels his oats as a winner, there may be a dozen who are made to feel like losers, wearing lifelong marks."

—Joe Paterno, Penn State head coach

"For years, the colleges have been waging a bitter warfare against the insidious forces of the gambling public and alumni and against overzealous and shortsighted friends, inside and out, and also not infrequently against crooked coaches and managers, who have been anxious to win at any cost. . . . And now comes along another serious menace, possibly greater than all the others, viz. Sunday professional football."

—Amos Alonzo Stagg, 1923

"The only thing that keeps the NFL going is gambling."

—Alex Karras, ex-NFL lineman

"If I had had a knife, I would've stabbed him."

—Bears tackle Dan Hampton, after running back Brad Muster fumbled at a crucial point in a game

"Football is the only game you come into with a semblance of intelligence and end up a babbling moron."

—Mike Adamle, former Jets fullback

Index